HOW TO BE YOUR BADASS SELF

A Guide to Using Your Inner Energy for Brand Success

By: Annie Koshy

How to Be Your Badass Self:
A Guide to Using Your Inner Energy for Brand Success
www.findyourselfseries.com

Copyright © 2020 Annie Koshy

ISBN: 978-1-77277-362-0

Limits of Liability and Disclaimer of Warranty

The author and publisher shall not be liable for your misuse of the enclosed material. This book is strictly for informational and educational purposes only.

Warning – Disclaimer

The purpose of this book is to educate and entertain. The author and/or publisher do not guarantee that anyone following these techniques, suggestions, tips, ideas, or strategies will become successful. The author and/or publisher shall have neither liability nor responsibility to anyone with respect to any loss or damage caused, or alleged to be caused, directly or indirectly by the information contained in this book.

Medical – Disclaimer

The medical or health information in this book is provided as an information resource only, and is not to be used or relied on for any diagnostic or treatment purposes. This information is not intended to be patient education, does not create any patient-physician relationship, and should not be used as a substitute for professional diagnosis and treatment.

Publisher
10-10-10 Publishing
Markham, ON
Canada

Printed in Canada and the United States of America

| Dedication |

This book is dedicated to all the coaches, mentors, friends, and teachers in my life who have helped me through my journey into understanding myself. I am a better coach and mentor because I've been blessed with the opportunity to learn from the best.

I'd also like to dedicate this book to Raymond Aaron and his team, especially Tracy and Liz. Raymond, you gave me the courage to take what was in my head and put it on paper in the form of this book. I would be remiss if I didn't acknowledge that and dedicate this space here for my thanks for your guidance in making this dream come true. My lifelong gratitude to you.

| Acknowledgements |

To my two sons, Akshay (Shay) and Daniel. You are and will always be the most precious and priceless gifts to me that God has blessed me with. Remain safe and blessed. Live your dreams and always reach for the stars. I love you yesterday, today and always.

To my parents who have instilled in me a work ethic that has formed the foundation to me. Honesty, integrity and determination along with a grit and tenaciousness to consistently work at something till it is successful. You had high faith based expectations and that was the example you set for me. Thank you for giving the best of your life to making sure I always had the best.

Mahesh S., Ravi S., Ballo H., Tony S. and Satish Verma, the universe has conspired to bring us together. Thank you for your gentle, kind ways in how you encourage, motivate and unconditionally accept me, so I can be the best version of myself. You are gifts God has blessed me with when I least expected it. I love you yesterday, today and always.

To my two childhood friends Kelly and Sheeba. You have been firm advocates about ensuring that I'm living my dreams, listening to me without judgement, encouraging me in my moments of despair and laughing with me through so many crazy moments. In my crayon box of friends, you are the two colours that I chose the most because your colours are staples in my life. I love you both beyond any measure.

To all my friends who have become family. You stood by and cheered me when I didn't have the ability to cheer myself. I want to acknowledge how important you have been to me and how important a role you played in the journey to my success today. A special thank you to my childhood youth group who gave me a faith based foundation in friendship. Thank you for all your love.

| Foreword |

While there are books on personal branding available, none of them tackles the subject with as clear and tangible actions items as *How to Be Your Badass Self: A Guide to Using Your Inner Energy to Build Brand Success.* In this must-have guide, Annie Koshy shares the knowledge she has gained about building a personal brand from growing her own media business.

Right from the start, Annie gets you focused on what your strengths are, and how you can maximize them as part of your branding strategy. *In How to Be Your Badass Self,* Annie also dives into your mindset, recognizing that how you talk to yourself is key to building success in your professional career. Plus, Annie dives into how your thoughts are key to creating action and meaningful change.

Then, Annie shifts to the practical aspects of building a brand, from choosing a logo to understanding how color plays a part in making emotional connections between potential clients and your brand. Critical to every aspect of this process is consistency. Annie breaks down how critical consistency is, in every aspect of your personal branding and marketing strategies.

Annie also dives into how building the right habits can reinforce your vision for your personal brand. Along the way, she also shares inspiring stories of how building on failure, encouraging creativity, and thinking outside of the box can lead to amazing growth in your badass personal brand. Finally, explore how you can be the best brand ambassador, building a positive professional image to develop your relationships with other professionals and clients.

No matter where you are in your professional career, *How to Be Your Badass Self: A Guide to Using Your Inner Energy to Build Brand Success* is your reference guide to taking your career to the next level and becoming the badass you were meant to be!

Raymond Aaron
New York Times Bestselling Author

| Table of Contents |

PRO TIP

anniejkoshy.com

"When you change things within you, what you surround yourself with also changes.

Don't stop.

Keep upgrading yourself with new skills, positivity and determination."

ANNIE KOSHY - AUTHOR
HOW TO BE YOUR BADASS SELF
A Guide to Using Your Inner Energy for Brand Success

CHAPTER 1
WHAT'S YOUR STORY –
THE PERSONAL
BRAND

| **Chapter 1 -** What's Your Story – The Personal Brand |

| **Why is personal branding important?** |

"Who am I?" you may ask. What do I have to share with you that will help you? Nothing that you don't already know. Nothing I have to say in this book is rocket science or something you haven't heard and tucked away in the recesses of your mind. This book is only good if you're ready to take stock of what you already know and truly apply it. Are you able to truly crash and burn, and build yourself up from those ashes to become your best self?

The journey you will be on will be personal and unique, requiring action. What I have done and accomplished is based on my own unique journey and the actions I was willing to take to achieve my personal and professional vision. You can do the same, by beginning to apply some of the tips and tricks shared here. This is how I took my own brand from non-existent to a household name. Join me as I explore each chapter and share some of my insights on my last five decades, on how I became my own "badass self!"

Personal branding is a process by which you create a public persona to market yourself or your business. Why is this important? Determine whether you wish to be blah and mediocre, or stand out and apart from the crowd. A determination to stand out is why personal branding is key.

In an age where everyone is using social media to market themselves, their products, and their services, we are constantly inundated with content, both relevant and irrelevant. Having your own impactful personal brand puts the spotlight on you, in a sea of mediocrity. It showcases your strengths, garnering interest and attention to your business in a positive manner.

Building a personal brand creates credibility, authenticity, and helps garner trust in your interactions, both personally and professionally. Establishing credibility in any given field is essential if you want clients to believe in you and your services. Having a personal brand that is consistent to your goals and services helps build that trust, which is essential for the growth of any business.

If you can't build trust, then you are putting the pressure on your business to constantly be recruiting new clients, which is extremely costly. Building trust is much more effective as it is easier to keep a repeat client than to make a new one. How can you build trust through your personal branding?

Begin by being your authentic self. The revelation of who you are, and your unique style, helps to build brand loyalty. When you unleash the power of your authentic self, the energy released is powerful. This palpable force builds an aura around you that continues to benefit your business.

Let's reflect on some of the major corporations that currently exist. The force of an authentic personality often defines the brand. Apple and Steve Jobs, Amazon and Jeff Bezos, or Virgin and Sir Richard Branson—all these men have defined the brands of their companies, and the auras they have created still live through their businesses to this day.

The development of your personal brand can accurately share your values, goals, and purpose. Achieving your personal brand is not something that happens by chance or is an overnight success. What seems effortless takes years of practise, trial-and-error, and a determination to succeed. However, before you can effectively convey your personal brand, you need to understand what you bring to the table in terms of marketable value.

| How to Find Marketable Value in Yourself |

When people get stuck in moving careers, especially those in the higher administration, such as CEOs and vice presidents, the question, "What do you do?" seems to stump them the most. After all, the answer is usually that they run a company, but often these individuals have lost sight of their value. It could be their gift for strategic vision, or simply their ability to marshal resources so that they are utilized effectively. If you cannot articulate the gifts, talents, and skills that contribute to your value as a leader, then how are others expected to see them?

I find that those in high positions get accustomed to doing multiple tasks throughout the day, moving from one department to another, handling the fires, and making hard decisions. In the process, they lose sight of what they are truly good at and what makes them uniquely fit, to do their job. Essentially, they lose the ability to explain exactly what they do and how they do it.

Finding the marketable value within yourself is about having a clear understanding of who you are and what you bring to the table. After all, how will others find value in you, if you don't find value in yourself? It is not up to those individuals you meet to define you and your skills. Defining your marketable value is one of the first challenges to create a branded persona. Identify your value by determining:

- What You **KNOW** How to Do – Qualifications
- What You **CAN** Do – Positions held
- What You **LIKE** to Do – Hobbies, things that bring you joy/ happiness

The first two are quite straightforward, as these are the skills and qualities and achievements to date. What you know how to do is your knowledge base; the foundation of your marketable value based on your qualifications. What we know how to do comes from the experiences and knowledge we have gained from them, either formally or informally. The positions and achievements you have held also contribute to that knowledge base.

Often, these are the skills you know you can do, because you have done them in the past and you can prove it.

The last question is an area we have to look at more closely to really understand what we truly want to do. What you like to do can be harder to define, because it is based on the things that you like to do and find joy in, and those experiences and moments that bring you happiness, which may not necessarily have a cut and dried professional connection. Ideally, what you would like to do should also include a combination of what you know how to do and what you can do.

What holds us back?

Either we have limiting beliefs, or we don't know how to make our unique knowledge, experiences, and skills marketable. We self-talk ourselves into believing that we can't do what we like because of a plethora of excuses. Here are just a few:

- We aren't good enough.
- We aren't wealthy enough.
- We aren't big enough.
- We aren't tall enough.
- We aren't pretty enough.
- We aren't smart enough.
- We aren't educated enough.

The list can go on and on. When we start looking at what holds us back, and begin to break these shackles, then our thoughts begin to align with what we would like to do. The biggest challenge for many individuals is finding a way to monetize what they love to do. A hobby is not a business until you can make money out of it.

The challenge is to find a way to break down those barriers that may be holding us back. These limiting beliefs stop us from fulfilling what our true desires may be.

If you are dealing with limiting beliefs, then your challenge is to identify them and work to change them. While that might not be easy, it is possible with a conscious and consistent effort.

| Making a Living Doing What You Love |

If you are struggling to find a way to monetize or make what you love, marketable, then you might need to think outside of the box. Too often, we are told that something is impossible, simply because no one had ever done it before.

Look around on your phone. There are so many things that you can do with the swipe or touch of your finger. In just a few minutes, you can connect with individuals around the world, make purchases, and more. All of this that we can do now with the mini-computer in our hand, was considered impossible just a couple of decades ago.

Your limiting beliefs can be keeping you from creating the next "impossible" thing for the public to utilize. Exploring what you enjoy is about looking at what sparks your creativity, and finding a way to connect your career to that passion.

Once you are able to determine what you like to do, then when you look at what you've done and what you can do, the picture starts to look a little different. Essentially, you are now combining all the knowledge and skills that you bring to the table. It can provide a completely unique picture of your marketable value. It might even amaze you to figure out what you may have forgotten that you were capable of accomplishing.

Determining your value depends greatly on how you look at yourself, and not really on what external factors may determine to be your value. I am a strong believer in the idea that if you don't value yourself, then how can you expect others to find value in you? You need to stop undermining and/or limiting your own value. When you see yourself as valuable, that translates into a confidence and respect in the marketplace. Don't be quick to dismiss how much that can positively impact your personal branding.

I know what my worth is and what I am able to deliver, and I know what I should be receiving, based on what my marketable value is for the type of work and number of hours I put in. Now when people reach out to me, they are willing to meet my expectations. When I started raising the value for myself, other people started valuing me even more for my work. As a result of valuing myself, the work I do has a higher marketable value. If you are able to determine your work and the worth, then you can set the value for your work, right from the get-go.

| How to Communicate Effectively for Branding |

It is about determining and articulating your expectations, as well as understanding the expectations of others. When I drafted a proposal for a client, I referred back to notes I had taken during our initial meeting. Those notes included some of the challenges that they were facing. My proposal addressed those three main areas of concern that they had, reflecting the fact that I heard their concerns and worked to address them.

I started off with what their challenge was, and then proposed the solution that we had to offer. I maintained that consistency throughout the proposal. Then when I talked about pricing, it went right back to the challenges they were facing, and the price reflected what it would take to resolve that challenge.

Again, everything was consistent. It immediately established my company brand and what I am able to deliver. I shared what my clients could expect from me, and showed how my services and products could meet their expectations of this relationship.

Communicating effectively needs to be done across all levels of documentation, including marketing. The goal is to set out a clear vision for your clients, one that is easy for them to understand and follow. Effective communication is key because it defines your unique personal brand!

If I had been vague in my proposal, then it would not have accurately or effectively communicated what I wanted to do in order to answer their specific challenges. When you look at your presentations or proposals, are they accurately reflecting your personal brand? Or are they vague, making it difficult for your clients to understand your message, thus setting the stage for misunderstandings and frustrations?

However, it can be challenging to stay consistent when you are not sure what makes you special or what makes you stand out from the crowd.

| Finding Your WOW Quotient |

What is your WOW quotient? Essentially, this is a characteristic or set of qualities that makes you stand out or gives you the edge. What is the one thing you do that no one else can do? What is unique that you bring to the table?

Part of the answer to this question is wrapped up in understanding your marketable value. After all, if you understand what makes you valuable, it can be easier to identify your **WOW** factor. The main point to remember is that all of this contributes to you making a badass first impression. You don't get another chance to make that first impression.

When I get ready to head out on stage, every step along the way is part of creating that **WOW** for my audience. That establishes the basis for everything they will experience in my presentation. I come out as a finished product, ready to begin. There are no excuses, hesitations, or reasons why I need just a few more minutes. I am ready to go, and that energizes them before I even open my mouth. That creates the WOW that creates a great first impression. No matter what is happening behind the scenes for me, the audience doesn't know anything about it. Once I'm on stage, everything is smooth and scheduled. I have a genuine smile on my face, and my confidence and personality spreads to my audience. It is so important to have that WOW, and to build it into your own personal branding.

*So how do you determine your **WOW** factor?*

Ask yourself the following questions:
- What makes you stand apart from others that are in your circle?
- How do you walk into a room and make an impression that you've arrived?
- How do you create a lasting impression once you leave?

One of the essential components of building your personal branding is developing your capacity to create a brand that holds value and relevance. If your clients don't see the relevance in what it is that you offer to them, your products and/or services hold no value. No matter how great your idea or purpose is, they will be very unlikely to follow through with any purchase, or come back to you for your business.

Your **WOW** factor is about helping you hold your value by keeping yourself relevant. However, many branding ideas focus on doing what everyone else is doing, as if that is all you need in order to have a viable personal brand. Online marketing has grown, along with the birth of social media.

Now there are a variety of professional platforms that people use to connect with others in their industries, as well as potential clients. Just putting up a few posts is enough, because they are keeping up with the crowd.

Building value in your brand is something that you can't just do based on a website. A **WOW** factor is based around the idea of standing out, not just doing what everyone else is doing. A **WOW** factor means being able to acquire customers, then being able to retain them while representing your core values. Be your own core value brand ambassador when speaking to your clients about what it is that you do. One of the things that you have to ask yourself is what people value in you. What is it that people see as your strengths? What do they find that you have that really draws them to you?

No matter what your **WOW** factor is, by highlighting it throughout your branding, you are taking your professional brand to a new level.

| The Consistency Factor |

Once you figure out what makes you stand out, or your **WOW** factor, it is important to maintain consistency in your branding and communications to reinforce that. The consistency factor is key to building your business. In my proposal example, I focused on not only providing them what they needed to answer their challenges, but I presented it in a way that was easy for them to follow, from the proposed solutions to the pricing. Nothing was out of place, simply because I made consistency a priority. I am a walking logo for my brand.

Is your personal branding suffering due to a lack of consistency? Your branding might be well communicated, but does the message appear to change with every new piece of marketing? Are your core values and ideas able to be understood, or does your branding seem to leave more questions than answers?

The reason that you need to become consistent is because that consistency will contribute to the level of trust that your clients feel with you. Plus, your clients need to know what they are getting every single time they interact with your company. They shouldn't be surprised, and it contributes to your marketable value. If they get a great experience one time, and then a horrible experience the next time, they will be less inclined to hire your services, or purchase your products. In fact, their mediocre interaction with you or your brand may actually bring your marketable value down when sharing their experiences with others.

You will hear me mention this frequently throughout these chapters. It is vitally important that you recognize how consistency can either benefit your branding or sink it. Whatever your target audience is, they need to be receiving your core message.

Your identity, values, and strategy, over time, have to be very homogeneous. It is very important that whatever your core messaging is, that your target audience is receiving that messaging and seeing all the elements reflect that messaging uniformly. My brand colors, for example, are red, black, grey, and white. You will invariably see me wearing those colors, especially when I am speaking or doing a show. Even in that small element, I am being true to type with my brand messaging. I am subliminally tying them to my logo. Although people don't realize it, every time they see me, they are connecting that with my logo, or visualizing my logo. I am a walking brand of my logo.

The core values of my brand remain uniform with the elements that my target audience see and hear from me as well, as they are exposed to my brand visually and help build that brand connection. So that brand consistency is a vital aspect of spreading that brand messaging.

With that in mind, let's talk about another area where consistency can play a role, and that is the people you surround yourself with.

| Surround Yourself With the Right People |

Recognize that whoever you are surrounding yourself with are going to impact your marketable value. If you are spending time with individuals who are not motivated, not focused, and not trying to learn and grow, then those traits are going to impact you. If they are not trying to reach the same level of success and financial freedom, then there is no way that you are going to be able to push yourself to the next level. They will become an anchor around your neck.

You need to surround yourself with people who are succeeding at the level that you want to reach. They are going to motivate you to step up your own game, so that you can reach that next level of success. You are going to start pushing yourself even further and harder, with the results being that you achieve your vision for your career. Both who you know and who you surround yourself with are going to play a key role in how you approach your marketable value.

Just like in a tennis game, if you play with someone better than you, your game will improve. Always have people who are mentors, who have done it better than you, or have achieved what you want to achieve, surrounding you. Listen to them. Get into your car and listen to that podcast. Read their articles, blogs, or books. You need to be constantly immersing yourself with information about where you want to get to, and that coincides with your path of growth as well.

If you hang from the monkey bars, you are going to get taller. The point is to stretch yourself, reaching for that top. We need to take that same attitude and put it into your mental growth as well. You should always be reaching for something higher, a goal that you are not quite there yet, but it is in reach if you stretch just a bit further. Go for it, because it is attainable. Get motivated and inspired by those who are also on your path. Do not set yourself up for failure by comparing your progress to someone else, and then telling yourself that you are never going to get there.

Reaching for those attainable goals and milestones, by surrounding yourself with positive messaging—from the people you spend time with to what you listen to and read—is what is going to get you to the next level. Those individuals need to bring a positive energy into your life, encouraging you and challenging you to keep reaching. Who is in the real estate in your head? That is so important. Do not put people into that real estate that are not going to fuel your growth. Surround yourself with the right people and the right messages.

As a parent, you are modeling how to learn and grow for your children. If you take an attitude that success is constantly learning and improving, and failure is simply a chance to grow, then that is the energy they will take into their lives. Imagine harnessing their energy and power in that positive fashion, and how much change they can create as a result!

I firmly believe that you can't get better if you don't play with those who are better than you. Challenge yourself by spending time with those who have already been where you want to go. Get motivated and inspired to make improvements, to learn and to grow. When you surround yourself with the right people, you will be amazed at how it changes who you are and what you believe is possible.

Key Takeaways:
- Creating a personal brand is key to having the career and life that you love!
- Be consistent to achieve your goals.
- Define your WOW factor and capitalize on it.
- Surround yourself with people who are better, to learn and grow.
- Stretch yourself personally and professionally to reach your goals.

Clearly, a personal brand is key to becoming the badass person you were meant to be. Still, before I share how to become a badass personal brand, let's talk about how your thoughts contribute to your success!

PRO TIP

anniejkoshy.com

MIND STRENGTH

"When you channel your mental strength, you can change how you think, feel and behave to ensure your priorities are in line with your beliefs."

ANNIE KOSHY - AUTHOR
HOW TO BE YOUR BADASS SELF
A Guide to Using Your Inner Energy for Brand Success

CHAPTER 2
SEEDING THOUGHTS – USING MIND STRENGTH TO FUEL CHANGE

| **Chapter 2 -** Seeding Thoughts – Using Mind Strength to Fuel Change |

Every time I lift my camera to my eye, I find myself marveling at the power of the camera. A picture is worth a thousand words, capturing a moment in someone's story. Later, when looked at, these memories are filled with many missed details captured by these images. Exploring my personal creativity through a camera has allowed me to connect with people in amazing ways. I see them at their most vulnerable, their happiest, their saddest, and I see their joy and their love. Then I capture that moment in time with the push of a button. It is a powerful moment. Then there are those beautiful landscapes, which challenge my skills but bring me pride and joy every time I look at them. There is power in exploring your environment from behind the lens of a quality camera.

In the same way, the beauty of our minds is in the amount of power that it possesses. You can shape your lives through your thoughts and emotions. What you focus on becomes a part of your life, whether it is positive or negative. These thoughts give us the ability to change our lives, because we are not stuck with our mindset. You have the potential to create, and it starts by acknowledging the abilities and power found within your mind. It starts by acknowledging your thoughts and how they can impact your life in ways large and small.

Harnessing the power of your mind affects everything that you do. In fact, it is actually the most critical part of being able to make change the way that you want to make change. Therefore, let's zero in on how to harness that power in a meaningful way.

| Harnessing the Power of the Mind |

When it comes to harnessing your mind's power, you need to give yourself a little **FLACK.** Let's break down what that stands for and come to a deeper understanding of what it means in your personal branding.

Find Your Purpose - Finding your purpose starts by identifying what you are passionate about. It is about knowing and understanding what makes you happy and then pursuing it. What makes you joyful or gives you the zing to get up in the morning and tackle the day? When you are able to identify that, and you are able to focus on that, then it becomes the first thing you think about in the morning, and the last thing you think about at night. Your purpose literally ends up permeating through every aspect of your life. That's when you know that you have found your calling, the thing that you really want to do. It is the voice in your head or in your heart, when you are quiet, that really does speak to you. It is in those moments that it lets you know if you are really on the right path. That voice helps you to know if you need to make a change or if something is not going right in your life.

This is the voice that tells you "Bingo!" indicating you are on the right path. Those are the messages that your subconscious, subliminal mind is sending you. We need to pay attention to these voices to be able to hear what our purpose is. Once you are able to identify your purpose and what makes you happy, keeping that in focus and in alignment will be the first step to harnessing the power of your own thoughts.

Learn How to Please Yourself, Not Others - One of the realities of pleasing others is that if you are not careful, you can end up being controlled by what others think or want. Their expectations can end up guiding your life, putting you in the position of pleasing them before you do what makes you excited and joyful.

I come from a background where serving others is emphasized. As women, we often find ourselves serving or working to please multiple people within our lives, whether that be our partner or spouse, our children, our parents… and the list goes on and on. Often, we put their needs above ours, thus lessening the value of caring for and loving ourselves. There are even moments of guilt if you spend money or time on yourself. There is often a lack of balance in families and relationships, where women are called on to sacrifice more for the greater good. However, that comes with a heavy price for the women, who are often left drained— mentally, physically, and emotionally.

Doing things for ourselves becomes a guilty pleasure, and we need to stop that assumption right now. It is not a guilty pleasure, but a critical one to our own sense of purpose, equilibrium, and sense of happiness. We need to be able to tell others, "You may not find value in it, but this is valuable to me." Those conversations need to be had, so that we can avoid being judgmental based on what we think is valuable, and judge others based on that. Additionally, when we shift our thinking, we stop asking those around us to find value in us and what we do. Instead, we find that value for ourselves, internally. Then we can do things for ourselves just for the sake of doing them, instead of choosing to do or not do things based on the response or negative energy we receive from others.

Often, as wives and mothers, we think that by sacrificing to such a large degree for our families, they can be happier. The reality is that by not putting our own happiness first, we are actually not making anyone else happy. It is about taking a step back and figuring out what makes you happy. When you are happy, then you can give off that energy and balance to others.

This is where you really tap into the power of the mind. What is the power of the mind? It is about being in that balanced moment of Zen, having that equilibrium within you to take the ups and downs of what is happening around you and not let that really sway you.

Think of yourself as being anchored on a ship, which is constantly swaying and rolling about. If you have your feet firmly planted, then you can go with the rolling sensation of life to keep balanced.

Being happy within yourself and doing things to make yourself happy gives you that inner balance and an inner sense of peace. When you have that, you are like a magnet to others, and they will be able to see that calmness within you. That is your power and the gift you give to others.

However, to truly benefit from this, you must break years of ingrained habits that focus on pleasing others first. It is about breaking the habit of explaining why you are doing what you are doing, or why you made those particular choices. You do not need outside approval to validate your choices or to confirm that you can be happy now. You do not need to apologize for your actions or decisions. Making the transition is challenging, but it is key to finding your happiness and joy.

Often, when we look back to see what has happened in the past, we have two options. You can get stuck in the quagmire, similar to quicksand, where you put your foot in and just keep sinking. Essentially, you are reliving what has happened, envisioning what could have happened, and immersing yourself in the emotion of it. Even talking about it can make you feel as if you are trudging backwards into some form of misery. On the other hand, if you look back at your past, acknowledging that it happened, and the places where you might have failed, then you have the information you need to identify where changes need to happen. What are you going to do today that you didn't do yesterday?

What has happened in the past is a point of reference and not of failure. What will happen in the future is yet to be fulfilled. Live for today. For the moment. For each experience. Be in the present.

Your past is a stepping stone, not a stumbling block. It should be a combination of moments where you made a pivot, recognizing what wasn't working for you, and redirecting your path.

Then you are living today while utilizing the lessons from the past. Another aspect of this is the future. We can get fixated on worrying about what is going to happen tomorrow, next week, next month, or even next year. We are worrying about the afternoon when we haven't lived in the morning.

Of course, it doesn't mean that you are living in some fairy tale world where everything is just magical and wonderful all the time, where you aren't thinking of the future at all. Instead, you are thinking of the future, but not trapping yourself in the future, allowing it to dominate your life right now. You are living in the moment and experiencing that moment. Then you are able to experience the fullness of that moment and experience.

For example, it is important to put everything else to the side and concentrate on what you are eating when you are eating, because it is fueling your mind and body. It is critical to live in that moment, not having your mind distracted by what has happened in the past or what could happen in the future.

Recognize that we have all made mistakes in our past. I don't think there is a single one of us who can say that they have nothing in their past they wish could be changed. I personally have made so many mistakes in my past, and there are so many things that I would have done differently, but I don't wish that I could have a do-over. Rather, I look at these experiences and focus on what they taught me. This is what I learned and how I applied it to benefit myself. When you take those lessons from the past, intercept them, and then use them to figure out what changes you need to make, then it is amazing how you can harness your power!

Start by looking at what you didn't like about yourself in that situation. What could you have done differently? What changes can that prompt for you? You are constantly honing and changing aspects of your life and your approach, based on the lessons from your past. All of these things help us to redefine our purpose and to clarify our path.

It is about aligning our thinking to bring up that equilibrium and mental balance that leads to the inner peace that we require.

Accept and Adapt to Change - One of the hardest things to do is to accept criticism, whether it is constructive or not, wanted or unwanted; our hackles often rise when someone says something to us that is not in alignment with what we had in mind. Now, this reaction also comes in varying degrees. If it comes from a person that we highly respect, then we feel more inclined to listen to what they have to say. If the person saying it to us is someone who we do not like, we are more inclined to be on guard and resentful for the advice.

When you get feedback from others, you need to be in control of and harness the power of your response. If the feedback is something important, and you feel within yourself that it is something that resonates with your message or thinking, then you can take that in and consider a change. Acting on feedback is not always necessary, but having a willingness to listen and to be open-minded is. Essentially, you are opening your mind to another perspective. In the long run, that will benefit you as a person, even if you opt not to make a change.

You don't have to just throw out everything that you have been thinking and doing just because someone shared their thoughts and viewpoint with you. However, there are often things that happen when someone gives you a perspective that is different from your own, thus allowing you to look at a situation from a different angle than your own. You are going to learn something that can help you to tweak your own brand and your own purpose. If you receive feedback, or criticism and adjustments are required, you have to set aside your own prejudices and prejudgments about the person who is giving it to you, and the situation or circumstances under which it is given. Do not be quick to become defensive, because that leads down the path of being close-minded. Opportunities for growth are missed when we neglect to open our minds.

Think about the actual content and words that were given, to see if they are applicable to you. That takes the power of the mind. It involves harnessing that ability and applying it in situations where you are given advice or feedback. Remember, we are given advice all the time, but are not always receptive to it, simply based on the perceived value of the person giving it to us. We need to be open-minded to receiving from beyond our circle of comfort.

This is a difficult point, and one that you might not be receptive to at first. You might be wondering why you should accept feedback from someone that you do not see as valuable in your life. Just because you do not see the value right now, does not mean that what they had to say is not valuable.

Personally, one of my triggers that can make me less receptive is the tone of voice that is used, which can positively or negatively impact how I receive the information, and whether I see the information as good or bad. Another trigger is my degree of respect for the person giving the feedback. If I don't respect the person sharing the advice, then it is going to be harder for me to accept it as valuable.

There are people in my life who have given me advice or feedback, which I resented or had a hard time accepting, but I know in my heart that what they shared with me was true and had value. We have all found ourselves in that position. It takes acknowledging our triggers and working around them to move toward the level of open-mindedness we need, to truly benefit from feedback or criticism.

Celebrate Your Success and Those of Others - This is one of the prime examples of why I started my own company. Within the media industry, we are often talking about what other people have achieved, and we celebrate them. Within our personal and professional spheres, however, we don't always do that. Many companies do not take the time to celebrate what their employees have accomplished, or the growth they have achieved. Why is this important?

When you plant a seed and water it, then you see the plant grow. The same is true with celebration. Stroking someone's ego can water it; by simply applauding or acknowledging, you are nurturing growth. The same can be said when you take the time to celebrate yourself and your accomplishments. The more positive an encounter, the more positive feelings you generate and release into the mind, then the more receptive you are to do all the other things we have discussed throughout this chapter, including adapting to and receiving change. All these things, and the portal to receive, open up in a positive way because you are exhibiting a positive mindset.

Positive thinking and a positive mindset have always proven to be more effective and faster ways to grow than when you receive negative reinforcement. Create positive interactions and focus on building relationships with those around you who help to harness your own mental power.

Know How to Control Your Emotions - This aspect focuses on understanding your emotional triggers, what causes them, and how to control them. It is not to say that you won't have those emotions, but to be able to control the emotion, rather than letting the emotion control you, is going to be very important. Often, when you change your pattern of behavior in a situation, from the way that you normally react, it changes the entire energy flow within that situation.

So, you find yourself having a conversation that does not seem to be going anywhere, or a battle with a sibling, child, colleague, or partner. If you look at what is triggering these patterns of behavior, such as conversation styles, and you do something totally different, then it disrupts the energy fueling that situation. It can really change the dynamics of that conversation.

Knowing how to do that, and how to control your ability to do that, is going to be paramount to harness that control over your mind, and to harness the power of control.

You are taking the reins back into your hands, and not giving those reins to something else. The resulting change can be significant, both in how you perceive a situation and how you are perceived by others.

Everyone's minds are unique and powerful tools that are often underused. We are such incredible energy sources. Once you find your inner energy source, you will just shine so much, becoming a beacon of light in your life and the lives of others. The reason we tend to gravitate to some individuals and not others, is often because of that positive vibe or energy that they give off. It is about the energy and the change they are willing to generate.

| Content Seeding |

When you think of a thought, then you give birth to it, and to the action that will eventually come from that thought. Eventually, from that action, it becomes a goal. Thinking a thought is one step; figuring out how you are going to do it is another and implementing that plan or completing the action is still another. These things are all aspects that will be important in *content seeding* your own thought process.

There are three important points in developing and changing your thought process, which together are known as content seeding. This is where you truly harness the power of the mind, taking all the other aspects we discussed in this chapter, and implementing them and giving voice to your thoughts.

- You think a thought, thus giving birth to it.
- You then nurture that thought and the action that will result.
- That now creates your purpose.

Finishing a thought is one thing; formulating how you are going to do it is another and embodying that action by completing it is the final piece.

These are all going to be critical aspects of shifting your thinking and harnessing your mental power. How can you content seed your thoughts?

First, look at what you are feeding your mind. Is it going to encourage and inspire you? Or is it a constant barrage of negativity? If you want to nurture thoughts that contribute to positive actions, then your mind needs to be open to receiving them. Content seeding is also critical to building your brand, something I will discuss in greater detail in a later chapter. For now, it is important to critically analyze what you are feeding your mind, because that is going to impact your thoughts and actions.

| Using Thoughts to Shape Action |

Since your thoughts shape your action, what you are dwelling on and allowing into your mind is going to fertilize your thoughts in a positive or negative way. The only way to change your actions is to change what you think and how you plan your actions based on those thoughts.

Earlier, I talked about dwelling on the past, worrying about what was already done and how it could shape your actions for the present, leaving you feeling stuck and not able to fully realize your purpose. My goal is to help you recognize how powerful your thoughts are, and to fertilize them with positive energy. Time and again, your thoughts will determine your actions. Learn from the past, but don't live there. Don't keep your thoughts trapped. Instead, claim the future by focusing on living in the moment and allowing your thoughts to be nurtured by positive energy.

When we choose a specific action or reaction, then we are sending off energy. Plus, our reaction can impact someone else's energy as well. If we look at how we are interconnected with all the different relationships in our lives, then we start to understand the different chain reactions we can create with the energy we give off.

Your one positive interaction can impact so many other interactions throughout the day. That becomes the power of mind over matter, the power of mind over negativity, and the ability to harness your power to create change in others. It helps you to fuel change in yourself and others.

| Tuning into Your Inner Frequency |

Time and again, the focus turns to the energy that you receive and the energy that you put out into the world. There are impacts from both sides. Your inner frequency is the vibe that you put out into the world.

Why is this so important?

Because your vibe is like a magnet. It will attract more of the same.

You may have heard the phrase, "magnetic personality." What is that?

Well, we all vibe at a certain level of energy. Think about the energy level that you have in the morning. If it is down, then you feel that throughout the day. People notice, and you might find that you are just not connecting with people, because your energy level isn't where it should be. You might even find people avoiding you, simply because they know that you are not in a good mood.

You are giving energy signals, and that energy is so important to harnessing the power of your mind. Along the way, you develop an understanding of what your personal inner frequency is and how to nurture it. You start to recognize when your frequency is off, and what you need to do in order to bring it back up to where it needs to be, to vibe at a positive energy level. This process goes back to controlling your emotions and understanding your triggers. Knowing your inner frequency is a key part in reaching your mental and emotional balance, falling in line with knowing and understanding your emotional responses.

| Developing a "Winning" Attitude |

If we wake up in the morning thinking that we will conquer the day, then we will conquer the day. However, if we wake up thinking that the day is going to conquer us, then it will do just that. Everything that we do during that day will be a challenge for us because our thoughts are focused on how challenging the day is going to be.

Attitude is everything! Regardless of what happens, if you wake up with a positive thought process and a winning attitude, then it will fuel all the interactions you have throughout the day with your partner, your children, your co-workers, and others. Essentially, each of those interactions will end up reinforcing your winning attitude, which will fuel your positive interactions. It becomes an amazing circle where your thoughts shape your reality.

Key Takeaways:
- Turn your thoughts to uplifting yourself, instead of dragging yourself down.
- Give yourself FLACK!
- Choose thoughts that lead to action, not excuses!
- Harness the power of your mind by understanding your inner energy frequency.

Give yourself a little FLACK, because it can help you harness the power of your mind, to grow both personally and professionally. You might be thinking to yourself, "Annie, I am open-minded; I accept feedback, and I am ready to be in the present. My struggle is defining what makes me unique in an industry where cookie cutter skills are good enough."

Have no F•E•A•R! Instead, face everything and rise. Your expertise is there, and it can be a powerful tool. Let's undercover what your expertise is and start capitalizing on it!

PRO TIP

anniejkoshy.com

KNOW YOUR OWN EXPERTISE

"You need to believe, value and understand your own area(s) of expertise before you can ask others to believe in you."

ANNIE KOSHY - AUTHOR
HOW TO BE YOUR BADASS SELF
A Guide to Using Your Inner Energy for Brand Success

CHAPTER 3
DETERMINING YOUR AREA OF EXPERTISE

| **Chapter 3** - Determining Your Area of Expertise |

Being badass in the entertainment industry is a must! It requires a high level of confidence and an incredibly thick skin, to not only survive but to thrive. You have to be grounded in your belief in who you are and what you are capable of producing, because I promise, there is going to be a line of people ready to tell you how impossible it is for you to reach your dreams and goals.

There was one audition that I went to, where the director was looking for a specific character type. Every part of the audition was nerve-racking, simply because his face and body language clearly indicated that I was done before I even got started! Despite that vibe, I was determined to make an impression. The result was that I got the part. I chalk it up to the fact that I didn't defeat myself by assuming that I had already lost before I even got started.

Time after time, I find myself reaching down into my belief in myself, and using it to keep moving forward, especially when I get rejection after rejection. No matter what the movies tell you, no one is discovered instantly. I certainly wasn't. It was going to audition after audition, learning, training, and honing my craft to come up with amazing performances, that got me to this point in my career. It was being open to experiences and capitalizing on my gifts, talents, and abilities that took me to the next level.

Part of this journey for me was learning what I did well, what I honed in on as my expertise, and then capitalizing on that. Sounds easier said than done, doesn't it? After all, we are called on to fill a variety of roles throughout our professional lives. You might be wondering what your expertise is. What do you bring to the table that is unique and special? Let's start by looking at the difference between what you know versus what you do well.

| What You Know Versus What You Do Well |

There are four main points to think about as we begin the discussion about your area of expertise. As a teacher, I would learn what I needed to know to teach that class before I went in. The night before or the week before, I would be prepping. However, I found that when I went in and taught the class, my knowledge of that subject was now solidified in a way that it hadn't been during all my preparation and review. My explaining the information allowed me to fully ingrain it into my thought processes. This goes for anyone who learns something and then shares it with someone else. You are solidifying your own knowledge.

By doing that, you are also going to receive feedback from your audience, regardless of their size. In my class, that audience was my students, and together, we would begin a conversation that allowed me to expand my understanding even further. You are constantly adapting and adjusting, being fluid so that you are always acquiring and building on your base of knowledge.
To do that, you participate in a back and forth, sharing knowledge and receiving it, adding to your knowledge base, and then sharing again. As you continue to do this, you develop a reputation of someone who is knowledgeable or who has become an authority.

That reputation means you are often consulted with, or you are the first person asked for advice on a specific topic or subject, simply because they see that you have acquired the expertise in that area. Thus, you establish yourself as a leader, thought guru, or expert.

Once you establish your value and the worth of what you know, then you can determine how that translates into monetary worth or professional value. Use that value to continue gaining additional levels of knowledge and expertise by expanding your professional connections. It becomes the clout that gets you to your next level.

If you are not a teacher, then what can you do to tap into this learning environment to build your expertise? Consider becoming a guide or a mentor. My personal mantra is that I surround myself with people that are my own mentors. Surrounding yourself with those who know more is one way to accelerate your own personal growth. You may end up being in a circle where you provide mentorship and guidance as you receive it.

Another method to build your expertise is by writing your thoughts down. There are multiple options, including writing a book, blogging, video blogging, or contributing articles to publications related to your industry. All of these are great ways to share your knowledge with the industry or profession. They don't have to be long articles, because many individuals are looking for something short and sweet that they can apply right away.

If your words end up becoming a quote that others share via social media, then you truly have become an expert. Whether you are a published author, through print or online, you attain a level of authority that translates into expertise.

To truly be an expert, however, it isn't just being quoted or having published your thoughts. It is about thoroughly knowing and understanding your area of mastery, then sharing that with others.

Establish your authority and expertise by training someone, as typically done through an apprenticeship. When you take on an apprentice, you are training and sharing your knowledge and experience.

Regardless of how you do it, sharing your knowledge helps on two levels. The first is your public speaking, because you must speak to share your knowledge. Many people find that a fear of public speaking is what holds them back from truly becoming an authority in their profession or industry. Being able to talk in front of someone else and share your knowledge is a great way to get comfortable with the idea of speaking in front of larger crowds.

Standing in front of a room full of people and sharing your knowledge and experiences is one common way to demonstrate your expertise.

The other area that develops your reliability as an expert is becoming a knowledge bank, being a point of reference for those looking for support. These are the primary areas in which you will be able to take what you know and do well, and share it with others.

| Concept Mapping to Determine Your Strengths |

We all have areas where we excel, or areas where we need to improve, as well as areas where our strengths and weaknesses overlap. Gone are the days where we pick a career and have that same career throughout the rest of our lives. Many of us will go through multiple careers during our adult lives. In this world of transitioning careers, transferable skills that can be applied from one career to another, are critical.

Take a look at your skills and knowledge. The goal of mapping all this out is to understand and lay out your strengths and transferable skills, such as your public speaking, writing, or organizational skills.

- What skills and knowledge overlap the various roles you held in your professional career?
- Was there a particular skill set that you weren't good at, but you learned and improved over time?
- What about your creative skills, such as graphic design?
- What about your technical skills, such as coding or programming?
- How good are you at managing customer outreach or sales?
- Are you strong in the area of number crunching?

The whole point is to lay everything out and determine where your strengths lie. A concept map will help you to better understand your strengths and the areas where you might find it easier to excel. Once you understand that, then you can find ways to translate those strengths into your next career choice.

Going down to the fundamentals and trying to build again isn't possible if you don't have the right tools to build from. That means before you can build anything, you have to go back and take apart anything that was not working. It becomes a burning cycle, where you have to obliterate what was there, and then build it back up from the ashes to create something new. The process can be painful, but the results are worth it.

| What Do People Come to You About? |

The other area that will help with listing your strengths and transferable skills is determining what people come to you about. In which areas do they view you as a resource?

One of the most important things is to be conscious of where your daily interactions occur in the work environment. Understand and balance the advice that you are giving, with observation. At times, advice can be thinly veiled criticism. Therefore, be judicious in how you share your observations and advice with others. Unless someone asks you specifically for your opinion, it is always better to err on the side of prudence. It is often the case that the advice you give may have more negative consequences than you intend; hence, the reason for caution.

Waiting for someone to ask you for the suggestion, or waiting for your observations to be requested, in a group discussion, is different from giving advice and balancing that with observation and judgement on an individual basis.

One of the ways that you can handle this is to ask if the individual is looking for suggestions or simply looking for a listening ear to share what they are going through. On a personal level, we tend to know what that person is looking for from us when they share what they are going through, and we respond accordingly. A lot of times, people may say something simply to get it off their chest, but not because they are looking for answers or input. In a work environment, to know if you can guide or mentor someone, you need to understand the boundaries of the relationship and not overstep them. If you are in a colleague to colleague situation, you should clarify if they are venting or asking for advice before you give any feedback or opinions.

Giving the other person the power of choice will give you more power in the long run. You give them the reins to lead the conversation, but you can then guide it using subtle questions.

| Determine Your Own Call to Action |

How do you decide, with all the things that you want to do, where to get started? My call to action in this book is based around why I am writing and the tangible takeaways that I want you to have at the end of it, including why these things are so important. My goal here is to impart information in a way that gets you thinking or shifting your mindset. It is about changing your viewpoint, helping you to view this information in a new and thoughtful way. If there is no call to action explaining why you are doing what you are doing, then those actions become pointless.

Your own personal call to action is defined by what is fueling you to do what you do. As an expert, what is it that you want people to do once you have shared your knowledge and expertise with them?

It could be that you want them to buy a product, subscribe to your podcast, attend an event, create a form, or submit some information.

Regardless of what it is, that call to action needs to be clearly grounded in what your purpose is and what you are doing.

Why do we not do the things we want or know how to do? I would argue that it is our own laziness or lack of a motivating force. Have a motive that will strike a chord within your audience to get them to do something different, to truly make a change. You must tap into their emotional response to get them moving toward changing their behavior.

It doesn't really matter what you are giving; the bigger issue is, what are they going to receive? Your call to action has to be something that they can buy into and will benefit from. Everyone is looking for their own personal gain. Behind whatever call to action that you put out there, is a reason why taking advantage of that is going to be beneficial for them. I know many people have heard of fear of missing out (FOMO). It is something that you can capitalize on to get people to heed your call to action.

Having people believe that if they don't act, they will lose that once-in-a-lifetime opportunity, can be a great motivator to get them to act. Retailers use this FOMO effect consistently during the holiday season or other peak shopping periods. Their goal is to make you feel the need to purchase right then, thus increasing your impulse purchases.

The other thing to look at, in terms of call to action, is to know how to analyze the social media tools that you are using, to determine whether the method for your call to action is actually fruitful. Google and Facebook both offer analytical options that allow you to see how many people are viewing, clicking, and sharing what you are putting out there.

Doing so will help you to adjust your call of action to grow those numbers effectively.

| Developing a Trust Quotient |

It is so important that trust be built through three key areas: how credible you are, how reliable you are, and how well you can connect with that person. When you have a combination of these three, then you have a level of trust. Different relationships have different levels of trust because it is not always necessary that you must like them to have their trust.

Think of an employee. You might not be their best buddy, yet you still have a level of trust with them, based on your authority and credibility.

At the same time, your credibility has little value with a family member or friend if you are not able to connect with them in a more intimate way. Your trust in that relationship is based on your closeness as people. Each relationship is balanced by these primary areas.

Additionally, when we look at the people around us, the gender differences regarding how we trust is also significant. For example, women tend to connect with other women on a much more personal level. They are more emotive with their connections. Women tend to be more articulate and willing to share, which creates another level of reliability. There is not the vagueness that comes into play with the phrase, "I'll get to it."

Our expectations regarding assertiveness in men and women is also shaped by society. Therefore, what defines the trust quotient can often be based on these societal expectations or preconceived notions. Recognizing how all these beliefs, expectations, and judgements play into your ability to gain the trust of your audience, is key.

As a result, building credibility and reliability is often necessary before you can build the clout and intimacy in your professional relationships. Through that buildup of trust, you can gain more power or clout in the long run.

Building skills and mastery can contribute to the trustworthiness of your relationships over time, unless you are in a position of authority right from the start. For instance, you might be promoted and have to trust in your management team until they prove themselves unreliable.

Your word is critical to building and maintaining trust with others and with your team. When you say something, follow through with it. Building trust through reliability and credibility is key to growing your brand.

| Be a Sponge for Growth |

I am constantly learning and growing by absorbing what is going on around me. The best way to grow as an individual is by learning and pushing your own thought processes to the next level. You have to surround yourself with things that are important for your mental growth. It all has to do with going to seminars, listening to that podcast, or reading that book. There is no point in listening to the doomsday news channel that focuses on what is wrong with the world. If you are able to change your mindset and fill it with a focus on how you can change the lives of those around you, then you are starting to make a difference.

Consider the real estate in your head as prime property, and treat it accordingly. Only fill it with things that will benefit you and help to grow your mindset. I personally have chosen not to have cable or watch television. In the car, I spend my time listening to music and podcasts, or I am making calls. It is about effectively utilizing my time to get the most out of it.

The time I take for my personal growth throughout the day is about expanding my own mind, growing my own self, growing my thoughts, and fortifying my own base knowledge so that I am able to share that in a more credible manner. When you look at your day, are you taking time to grow yourself? It is impossible to continue to be a teacher if you are not willing to be a student.

Key Takeaways:
- Establishing your expertise involves completely knowing your subject, mastering it, and then sharing that information with others.
- Use concept mapping to determine your strengths and areas of expertise.
- Focus on using the tools available to determine the effect of your call to action, and adjust as necessary.
- Be a sponge of knowledge, constantly open to learning and growth.
- Building credibility and reliability is critical before you can build clout and intimacy in your professional relationships.

Making time for learning and growth starts by the habits that you allow to dominate your routine, using up your time and energy. Let's talk about what habits mean for your mindset.

PRO TIP

anniejkoshy.com

THE AUTOPILOT

"When you have a
clear goal that
matches your
beliefs and you
create a set of
consistent actions,
you have switched
to autopilot."

ANNIE KOSHY - AUTHOR
HOW TO BE YOUR BADASS SELF
A Guide to Using Your Inner Energy for Brand Success

CHAPTER 4
AUTOPILOT YOUR PROCESS

| **Chapter 4 -** Autopilot Your Process |

My day can't begin without my hot water over roasted cumin seeds. Many of you might have coffee as your go-to morning drink. I am sure that there are a number of you out there who just live for the moment when you lift that steaming cup to your lips, inhaling that amazing scent right before you take that first delicious sip. Now that being said, I have a hot water machine. Every night, before I hop into bed, part of my nighttime routine involves filling the machine with water, preparing it for the next day. The next morning, I awaken and enjoy the fact that the water is ready for me to make that first refreshing cup. It is a habit, one that helps set up my morning to get off to the right start. However, one night recently, I got busy with several tasks and forgot to set it. The next morning, there was no hot water waiting to greet me.

My morning routine was totally thrown off, and it negatively impacted my energy level as I started my day. My habit, being disrupted, altered the rest of my morning routine. I did get something on the way to my first appointment, but that threw an additional errand into my day; and it meant that I had to factor leaving earlier, into my schedule. When my routine goes smoothly, then I am ready to tackle the day. When it doesn't, then I just feel like I am struggling to accomplish anything or to stay on track.

My mindset was shifted from the positive to the negative, and it took a conscious effort to shift back into a positive mindset for the rest of the day. Has this ever happened to you? Our habits become so automatic, yet they have so much power over how we approach our circumstances and the events of our daily lives. Habits shape our thoughts, emotions, and actions. Let's talk about how habits can create your mindset, and how you can use them to create meaningful change, personally and professionally.

| How Habits Create a Mindset |

There are several steps that help to create a changed or new mindset. One of the first things is how we talk to ourselves. Self-talk is something that can happen in our heads or even when we talk aloud to ourselves. There are things we say to ourselves when we are proud of our actions or efforts, and things that we say when we are disappointed or angry with ourselves. Regardless of why, the truth is that we are constantly focusing on these thoughts, this self-talk.

What we are telling ourselves could be holding us back. Once we identify it, then it takes work to turn that self-talk from a negative to a positive. It is about allowing our self-talk to help rather than hinder us from reaching our dreams and goals. If you believe that you didn't do something well, then focus on what you did do well, not beating yourself up unnecessarily for the things that you didn't achieve.

Changing your inner dialogue starts with your thought process, where you are actively concentrating on positive self-talk. Start by changing the language that you use when talking about yourself to others. If you tend to describe yourself by focusing on your mistakes or where you fail, then you are impacting how they view you, and creating a negative mindset within yourself. On the other hand, if you tend to focus on what you did well, rather than complaining about your own shortcomings, then you are encouraging others to build a positive mindset within themselves, and building it within yourself. I am a firm believer that positive builds positive. When you demonstrate a positive mindset in the language you use to describe yourself, then you are going to influence others to speak of themselves more positively as well. Changing your language is the second step in changing your mindset, the first being your internal thought process.

Once you determine the mindset you need to change, then focus on what you need to do to achieve that goal.

- What actions do you need to take, and what thoughts do you need to have?
- What is the process I need to get through to achieve that goal?

Look at a personal trainer. They didn't just wake up one day and find that they were a personal trainer. Instead, they went through a process of learning, achieving various milestones to accomplish that goal. It started with their own thought process and where they wanted to go with their own body shape and type. There were a series of small changes they accomplished, based on the larger goal that they wanted to achieve.

Essentially, you are forcing your thoughts to create an action that meets your goals. When you are doing these three steps, then you are learning and applying. The result is constant tweaking as you adjust based on what you learn.

When we do something, we are never going to be perfect at it. Therefore, you are constantly adapting to create a better outcome each time.

In the last chapter, we discussed the importance of mentors, and that is one of the themes that permeates throughout this book. You need to surround yourself with people who are going to help you step up your own game; those who might even have achieved your desired goal. You should hang out with those who have already achieved the success you want or are actively working to achieve that success, be it personal or professional.

When you start looking at what they do, and you start adapting to what they do, as well as to the feelings that they project, and following some of the earlier tips in this book, then your mindset is going to start to match your goals. Along that journey, you are going to create new habits.

Let's be clear; habits are not created overnight. Repeating the same action over and over again is what creates the habit. When you start doing something every day, and it becomes so natural that you do it without thinking, then you have created a habit.

The best time to grow in this regard is when you put yourself in an uncomfortable position. When you reach out of your depth and into an area where you need to challenge yourself, then you create the biggest mindset growth. You are challenging yourself for one of two reasons: either to survive or because you have reached rock bottom and there is no place to go but up.

When you face one of those two things and accept the challenge, then you are going to see that change in mindset happen.

| Intentional Change |

Who would you like to be versus who you are right now? What do you really need to do to step it up? First, you need to have a personal vision of who you want to be. There is your real self and then your ideal self. In previous chapters, I talked about the importance of creating a mindset by mapping your strengths and weaknesses, and then building on that.

- What are your strengths?
- What will your future self be like?
- What core strengths do you have right now that will help you to build toward that future self and that desired outcome?

Compare your desired self to your real self, and make the connections. Understanding your strengths and weaknesses is a start, and then adapting and adjusting based on constant learning will bring you up to that level. This part involves mapping out what you need to do to level up, and then actively working to achieve that.

Building the plan to achieve your desired outcome goes along with the action aspect. Breaking down the various steps toward your desired goal is your plan to achieve it. Sometimes wanting to be something or imitating an ideal mentor can be difficult to achieve overnight. It is important not to get out of your league by setting a goal that is unattainable. Instead, take small steps to keep you from feeling in over your head.

Looking at your ideal self, what contributes to making that ideal? The goal is not to overwhelm you but allow you to start writing out a plan. Give yourself an attainable goal, such as a maximum of five points that you want to work toward, and once you achieve them, then set another five. It becomes an ongoing process, but in the immediate future, you are only focusing on those five goals, which is a lot more attainable.

This process can be taken to your professional life as well. Prioritizing a task list is a common part of your day. Setting your goals, one or two things that you want to make a priority, can be done in the same way. Look at those goals, and create an action priority list.

- What is easy to do?
- What do you really need to work on?
- What is going to be challenging that will require a shift in mindset to get that action to happen?

On the other hand, you shouldn't be afraid to stretch yourself. Don't trick yourself into thinking that something is out of your league, and then decide not to try, when if you step it up, that goal could be attainable.

Positive self-talk involves encouraging yourself to stretch and make those choices that take you outside of your comfort zone. There are two different states of mind to remember. The first is the positive statements that nurture your own positive growth and the mindset necessary to achieve the goal of getting where you want to go.

Like you would encourage anyone else, then you need to encourage yourself. If you don't, then it can be difficult to achieve what you want to achieve. The second is to be the change that you want to see in yourself. Doing so can help you to keep going on your journey of changing your mindset, while positively impacting others.

| Fueling Your Own Personal High |

What does success mean to you? A lot of what determines whether we have been successful is based on the feedback that we receive from others. Coming from a personal and cultural point of view, if we have gotten a university degree and landed a professional job, such as a doctor, lawyer, or engineer, making a certain level of money, then you are deemed successful.

In the words of Albert Switzer, "Success is not the key to happiness. Happiness is the key to success." For me, I truly love what I do. That means I have a passion for it, and if I put the energy into it, then I will become successful. Money, status, and objective things, such as your home and possessions, are not a determination of success. There are many wealthy individuals who are not happy, and based on their material status, they should be happy—if we follow the model of success that society offers. Wealth is equivalent to success, which is considered equivalent to happiness. However, that is not always the case.

- What is success?
- Does that mean that anyone who is successful is happy?
- How do you decide what success looks like?
- Is it based on what others determine is successful, or is it based on your definition of success?

Success is best understood as doing what you enjoy and want to do, not what others determine you should do, or doing something because it will make someone else happy.

When you put the emphasis on what you value—on who you are, what you want to do, and what makes you tick—then everything else falls into place.

What I am telling you right now is not rocket science. Yet so many of us get up and go to a job that we hate, just because it is going to give us the money we need in order to pay for the things that we are responsible for, because that is what we all have to do. Even saying those words is monotonous and drudgery. It creates a feeling of "have to" instead of "want to." Who wants to live their life like that?

A lot of people are in careers doing jobs that they are miserable at, simply because that is what they are expected to do by their spouse, their parents, their friends, and even themselves. If they were able to do what they are really passionate about, however, I think the mindset of an entire society could be changed.

When you are doing a job, then you are fueling someone else's dream, not your own. When you are putting effort into making someone else happy and successful, but not making yourself happy in the process, then you need to lift up that ladder to success, and move it to another place that fuels your happiness and definition of success.

Defining what success means to you is a very important aspect of mindset. This is an evolving state, dependent on how other factors in your life impact your determination of whether you are successful or not. If it is very important to receive approval from certain elements in your life, be it your parents, spouse, friends, family, or employer, then that is going to impact your definition of success.

I had to go through several decades of my life before I realized that what other people determine as being successful, did not match my definition of successful. I needed to change how I approached it. When I decided that my mental state or my happiness was determined by what I enjoyed doing, and defined my level of success based on that, my personal mindset changed.

| Determine Your Habit Loop (Cue/Trigger - Routine - Reward) |

The steps needed to create change, which must be repeated over time, eventually become a habit. Once you create a habit loop, then you know that change has started to take place. When you start to make changes that become habits, then you are creating behaviors that will be lasting.

If you are doing this as part of a new mindset, then you are creating the changes that will elevate you as a person. How does this work?

The self-talk that I mentioned at the beginning of the chapter creates a mindset, telling yourself verbally the things that need to happen or that need to change. When you tell yourself that, then you are setting up mental and emotional cues in your mind, about how you are going to think. Over time, this self-talk becomes habitual. This is the first habit loop that you are going to make, which is your self-talk habit loop. It will become the foundation for so many others. You begin with a routine. When you wake up in the morning, then you say something to yourself along the lines of, "I had a great sleep last night." This could be a small target for someone, or it could be a huge target for someone who suffers from insomnia.

This three-step process involves creating a mindset, creating a routine based on that mindset, and then rewarding yourself for completing that routine. When you do so, then you are wiring it into your brain. That makes a loop.

If you want to get rid of negative self-talk, then start by focusing on what you did well, and praise yourself for that first. Then, look at what didn't go well, and focus on why it didn't go well and what change you can create to make it go better next time. This mindset moves away from berating yourself and diminishing your value. Instead, it focuses on learning, improving, adapting, and adjusting.

What are the cues you need in order to build the triggers for specific actions, thus creating the habit loop? When you look at a challenge or improvement from that perspective, then you are empowering yourself and shifting your mindset.

Habit loops are critical to turning on the autopilot within us. Although you need to be very conscious in the beginning, that autopilot will allow you to complete things without consciously thinking about it.

Turning on your autopilot can be associated with doing things mindlessly, by rote, and thus has a negative connotation. However, when I talk about autopilot, I am referring to turning it on once you have created good habits that you want to maintain. Automating the processes that I mentioned here helps to cement a mindset change.

There are a variety of autopilot habits that you may need to put into place. For example, how do you end a meeting? With all my clients, I end my meetings by scheduling the next one right then, and dropping in what we will be talking about for that next meeting—essentially a rough agenda. It is an automated process and serves me well. I have also automated putting any to-do list items that I need to accomplish before the meeting into my calendar. It makes the process smoother, and I am not trying to remember them later. If you do it right away, then you are saving time. These habit mindsets, which are so critical, are created when you start with the small changes that I have outlined. Automation builds consistency. When you start creating consistency within your own brand and behavior, then you start building trust with your clientele, and creating a reputation of being reliable. That is a critical step in creating branding success.

I am a firm believer that we are full of energy and create an energy field around us. Studies have shown that as humans, we vibrate on an energy level. When you start talking to yourself in a positive way, then you are aligning your energy with your true desire. That means you are starting to vibrate on an energy level that builds a mindset.

You are becoming more aware of who you are and what your needs and deepest desires are. When you are aligning your deepest desire with a true goal, then the actions that you are creating become easier to do. Putting those three steps together allows you to harness your energy, and you become more conscious of your thoughts and actions that create your new mindset.

One of the most important steps I had to take was to let go of the thoughts, actions, people, and situations that were holding me back. When you allow yourself to cut ties with the negativity in your life, the things that are holding you back, whether it is situations or a person you are involved with, or other self-limiting beliefs, then you start vibrating at a higher energy level, and you start to accept yourself and truly love yourself. You are allowing yourself to be happy. Happiness isn't a piece of clothing you put on, but a state of mind that can only be found within yourself. That is why there is a difference between someone who might not have anything in terms of physical wealth, but they are truly happy, versus someone who has everything in terms of physical wealth but isn't happy.

I am a firm believer that when your desires and energy are aligned, then whatever you put your mind to becomes more positive. When you are living the actions you want, then your goals become so visible that other people tend to gravitate toward that energy.

These people also seem to be more resilient. They have a mindset that they can get through anything. Achieving milestones is celebrated, both theirs and others. They can give of themselves without feeling drained. The quality of their relationships, productivity, and creativity all depend on this higher energy vibration and alignment. Your health will also blossom from this positive self-talk and energy. You will have an abundance in all areas of your life.

Key Takeaways:

- Determine where your mindset needs to change, and then create habits to support that change.
- Define what you believe is success, by determining what you enjoy doing.
- Allow your passion to fuel your actions.
- Choose self-talk that supports your changing mindset.
- Creating habits starts with a cue or trigger, a routine, and a reward.

Now that I have shared the importance of a positive mindset and opening yourself up to challenges, let's talk about how color and consistency play a part in building your personal brand.

| Notes |

PRO TIP

anniejkoshy.com

WEAR YOUR COLOURS

"I am red, black, white and grey.

What are YOU?"

ANNIE KOSHY - AUTHOR
HOW TO BE YOUR BADASS SELF
A Guide to Using Your Inner Energy for Brand Success

CHAPTER 5
WALKING YOUR BRAND COLOURS

| **Chapter 5 -** Walking Your Brand Colours |

Getting dressed in the morning is often a reflection of your mood. Wake up in a sunshine mood, and you are likely to gravitate toward colours and an outfit that magnifies that mood for you. A bad mood can be reflected in the colours and outfit that seems to amplify it. My bad mood outfits tend to make me look frumpy, and I feel ugly in them. My good mood outfits make me feel attractive and emphasize all the things that I love about my body. Notice that the outside becomes a reflection of the inside. Making the conscious decision to put on an outfit that makes me feel attractive and compliments me, even when I am in a bad mood, can often help me to mentally shift my mood. Now I am working from the outside in.

With that in mind, my personal branding on the outside is a reflection of my values, vision, and purpose. The colours of my logo can actually be tied to my messaging. It is not just picking the colours that I liked but picking ones that fit my brand.

When I went on the journey of branding myself, I realized that I needed to be consistent in all areas of my life to reflect my brand, even down to the colours and clothes that I wore. That is when I started thinking about the messaging behind the colours and how they impact us.

Brands choose colours and patterns that are immediately associated with them. I could literally name dozens of sets of colours, and you would connect them immediately to the brand. With that in mind, let's talk about the importance of choosing the right colours and how to create an association between your brand and those colours.

| Why Branding Colours Are Important |

Colours fuel us. There are enough studies out there that demonstrate the psychology of colours and how they impact us. I use colours to change my mood, but also as a reflection of my mood. Colours convey so much to me, even a specific smell and feel. I surround myself with colours that reflect what is important to me.

Sunshine is important to me, for instance, and so adding yellow into my life reflects that. I love the beauty of Mediterranean blue, and so it also finds its way into my life somewhere. My walls of my home are white and grey, reflecting the clean and calming impact of these colours on me. These are things that I have put into my environment, so it reflects the type of mood that I want when I am in that environment.

When I moved into my current home, the walls were a putrid yellow and very depressing. Painting the walls was one of the first changes I made. The shift made the environment more appealing to me. Why can those wall colours have such an impact on you mentally and emotionally? Much of it relates to the underlying messages of those colours.

| Subliminal Messaging Through Colour |

Your logo colours have underlying messages that can be conveyed about your brand. Let's look at my logo as an example and what I want it to convey to my target audience. Red is a vibrant colour and I find it to be very motivating. It is also balanced with black, which represents life and rebirth. White is a representation of freshness, which I wanted reflected in my logo as well. When I added the grey, then I had the calming influence.

Below are some of the meanings associated with each of the colours within my logo.

Red – Red stands for passion, excitement, and anger. It can signify importance and command attention.

White – White evokes cleanliness, virtue, health, or simplicity. It can range from affordable to high-end.

Gray – Gray stands for neutrality. It can look subdued, classic, serious, mysterious, or mature. For me, it signifies the necessity for me to listen and absorb what my client is saying, and to understand their needs without passing judgement.

Black – Black evokes a powerful, sophisticated, edgy, luxurious, and modern feeling. I personally love how it enhances the words within the logo, making them stand out.

I have noticed that black and red are two of the primary colours that I gravitate to, and they tend to reflect my own inner energy. I consider myself very sophisticated and educated, but I am also gracious in how I deal with others. There is a bit of a diva in me as well, reflecting the vibrancy of my nature.

My logo is significant because it also includes a photograph that I took of the city, which was made into a silhouette, and it has been tinted with various shades of the colours that I found important. It was critical to me that the message these colours conveyed was in alignment with the message of my business.

| Consistency Starts With Your Colours |

I am also very consistent throughout my branding in terms of colours and fonts. Anything that goes out officially from my company will always have my brand colours in it. If I am marketing something that I said or did, then I will try to use my brand colours. For instance, if I send a follow-up letter to a client, I ground that letter with the colours of my company logo.

The solid black, the vibrant red, the crisp white, and the soft grey all work together to reflect a consistency of message; and even if I don't add my logo, the message is still there. That consistency identifies me and my brand with the market, and develops trust that way. When I go out on camera for something specifically related to my company, then I try to make sure that I am in some form of my brand colours.

As I have been talking about the messaging that is created by colour, you might be wondering why that is so important. When you are advertising and marketing your brand, colour has a huge impact on what potential clients remember about your business. If you think of a brand like Coke or Nike, then you can easily picture the colours associated with their brands. Choose colours based on the image or emotion that you want to evoke in your audience or clients. Certain colours are cool, warm, and neutral. Deciding on a balance between those things will help your brand stand out, but also reflects your vision.

For instance, my logo is primarily made up of warm and neutral colours. I don't really have a cool colour in my logo, yet it reflects who I am and my personal energy.

Now, cool colours, which include blue, purple, and green, can definitely have their place. Corporations might use the cool colours to reflect different messages.

For example, finance companies and political conservatives tend to use blue in their logos. Here are just a few colours and the brands that you might immediately associate with them.

- Yellow and Green – John Deere
- Green and White – Starbucks
- Yellow – Best Buy
- Yellow and Red – DHL
- Brown and Tan – UPS
- Blue and White – Aerie
- Red – Roger's
- White – Apple

Each of these brands has created such a connection with those colors that even seeing them brings those brands instantly to mind. I can't help but think of how much consistency of brand colouring had to be done before large portions of the market began to associate these brands and their colours. Your consistency in colour use can bring about the same connection within the minds of your customers.

Those colours should permeate every aspect of your business, from your logo and letterhead to your website. The visual identity of your brand is based on the colour palette you use, the icons and graphics you choose, as well as the logo that you are developing. It is all shaped by your aura or persona.

| Associating Colours With Your Inner Energy |

With colours often reflecting your inner energy, as well as your brand message, choose colours that align with your personal energy.

Our energy is steeped with the colours that we vibrate with. My own aura's energy is brought to life with red, which reflects being a go-getter and having enthusiasm.

I have a very clear passion for life, and a desire to excel at everything that I do, and the red reflects that. The black reflects rebirth, as I have also felt that I am a phoenix, arising from an inferno. Grey reflects how I have been able to open myself up spiritually to enhance my intuition and creativity.

Let's take a second to identify your inner energy.

What colours do you most identify with? What do they say about you?

Now let's tie those colours into your logo. The result is likely a logo that gets you excited, because it aligns with who you are and ultimately, the message of your business. Letting a marketing person throw together their version of your logo, can often mean that it doesn't resonate with you or your brand, and lacks alignment with your energy.

| Understand Colour Subliminal Messages |

Your brand identity is conveyed through your logo and colour palette choices, which helps people get a feel for your brand. Choosing the colours for your brand logo helps to create a strong brand identity. Emote the messages that you want to convey, and then choose the colours that reflect them.

Colour psychology studies the hues of various colours and the perceptions that are associated with them. Those influences might not be obvious, but their influence can be found in the foods we choose to eat or even how we view a specific medicine. Part of understanding colour psychology is recognizing that the messages of a colour can be influenced by the viewer's age, gender, and culture. For example, men might find a red outfit more attractive on a woman, while the woman herself might not believe the colour had anything to do with why the man was attracted to them.

Another interesting point is that warm colours tend to attract spontaneous purchases, which can be a consideration if your business is retail. Even the choice of colour in building out your office or retail space can impact how your brand is perceived. Keep in mind that lighting can also impact how a colour is perceived, which can shift the message. For instance, red can also have a negative association with anger. To counteract that, I keep my red crisp, bright, and clean.

When choosing your colours, it is important to counteract any potential negative associations by using the colours to relay a positive message about you and your brand.

Customers or clients may often make a purchasing decision within 90 seconds of interaction with that product, with anywhere from 62–90% of that decision being based on colour. Victoria's Secret and H&R Block both used colour as a means to recreate their brand personality in order to target a specific audience. Some brands, such as women's shelters or spas, might end up creating their logo by taking into consideration the brands and companies they are associated with.

Therefore, I want you to define your brand message and what aligns with your energy to determine the right colours for your brand. To find the right colours, here are three steps to take:

- **Find your focus** – Whether you are rebranding or building a new business, you have to research what you are doing to build your focus.
- **Be open to change** – As you refresh your brand, you may find it necessary to change your colours up. That could also mean tweaking to make one colour dominate another as it relates to your brand.

- **Look at the competition** – Check out your industry and see the colours that they have used, and the balance between the dominant and passive colour choices. What has worked and what hasn't? It can help you to find the right mix of colours to create the optimal message for your brand.

A good ratio to keep in mind is the 60-30-10 rule. That means one colour will dominate by being used in 60% of your logo, with the other colours being divided by 30% and 10%. In my logo, since I use four colours, I have created the 50-30-10-10. However, the more colours you use, the more challenging it can be for your message to get across effectively. Using an endless number of colours can be overwhelming, so it is important to use a ratio to provide guidance in this process.

Take colour palettes or swatches from your local hardware store; you can actually combine different colours to get a look and feel of how they will interact with each other as part of your logo. It could help you to eliminate specific colours altogether and draw you to colours you hadn't originally thought of using. They can serve as a guide when you put your logo together. The end game of choosing your logo colours is about subliminally spreading your brand message to your current and potential clients.

Key Takeaways:
- Colours have emotional connections, so choose your logo colours carefully.
- Your logo and branding should reflect your energy.
- Once you choose the colours, make sure they are consistent across all of your branding platforms.

Throughout this process, the truth is that you are going to fail from time to time. Here is how I turned my failures into success and grew my brand in the process.

STEPS TO SUCCESS

"Every successful person has failed to succeed. Failures are the blueprint to YOUR success.

Walk On!"

ANNIE KOSHY - AUTHOR
HOW TO BE YOUR BADASS SELF
A Guide to Using Your Inner Energy for Brand Success

CHAPTER 6
MAKING FAILURES
YOUR SUCCESS

| **Chapter 6 -** Making Failures Your Success |

We have all had a moment in time when we felt like a complete failure. Whatever we had tried to accomplish had blown up in our faces. The feelings related to failure are horrible. It can have a terrible impact on our self-talk and so much more.

I remember not being very good at test-taking. Week after week, I came home from school with tests in physics, biology, and other subjects, with marks that were not up to the expectations being set for me. I would work hard, but my marks, in physics especially, were just above passing. It was horrible. Those negative statements I was telling myself, and being told by others, that I wasn't smart enough or I wasn't good enough, were simply not true. There were moments growing up, when I wondered if I was adopted, because it was just so easy for everyone else, and such a struggle for me. Then I graduated and got into a university program. That first year, my grades went from being mediocre to being in the high 90s. When that happened, I started to feel that I wasn't a failure, and that I did know something, and I wasn't useless.

It wasn't until I gained exposure to a career that captured my interest, that I started to realize true success. Much later in my life, I felt comfortable with the fact that I didn't have to live up to others' expectations of me. I started to applaud my accomplishments and didn't allow others to negatively impact me. I have come to recognize that all the work I did in high school was based on what people expected me to do in order to get lined up with the education and career that they expected me to be in. My success happened toward the later end of my career, when I started to explore the areas that made me happy, as I gained experiences and knowledge that I was able to put to good use in the businesses that I run today.

All of us have lived through moments where we felt the pain of failure. The question is, how are you going to use that pain and knowledge to grow toward success?

No Pain, No Gain – Using Your Experiences to Gain Knowledge

There are two ways to look at failures in life. If things didn't go the way you expected them to, or the way that others around you believe they should have gone, then that would be deemed a failure. Maybe you started a new job, took a class, or changed careers, and it did not go as you hoped. When we talk about success, as we discussed in Chapter 4, there are two determinants of whether you are successful: society and family, or whether you are happy in what you are doing. You internalize what success means, and then when those things happen in your life, you feel successful.

The overarching goal of this chapter is to shift your mindset from viewing yourself as having failed, to viewing it as increasing your knowledge and moving one step closer to where you want to get to.

If you don't work hard at what fuels your passion, developing and honing required skills, then you are not going to be able to truly master it. When everything comes easy with little struggle, then you never have the opportunity to challenge yourself, which is the only way for real growth. When you are uncomfortable and out of your depth, that is when you are really growing. To build your competence in anything, you need to fail and then grow from that. Becoming proficient at anything means reaching a point where you are stressed, and that stress pushes you and your ability in order to increase your competency.

In order for that growth to happen, you do need to fail. Anyone who has achieved personal or professional success, has likely failed more times than they have been successful.

That is how they have been able to further their interests, goals, and abilities. You can't become the best boat builder if you haven't built one that sunk. There is no way to be the best if you haven't learned from a total flop.

| Building From Setbacks |

Often, when we fail at something, the first reaction is that we are not good at it at all. There are several reactions to avoid falling victim to when you fail or deal with a setback. The first one is thinking that failure is the opposite of success. Failure is a moment for you to grow and to see where you need to hone, polish, or learn a new skill to get to that next level. It is a shift of your mindset, instead of a blockage. Failure is gaining knowledge, then walking away with more tools and experience for the future. Acknowledge what you think went wrong and how you might improve for the future. Doing so is a more proactive attitude to deal with failure and setbacks.

The other mindset to avoid is pretending everything is fine. When things don't go as we planned, and someone asks how we are doing, the first reaction is to tell them that we are fine. Although it is great to have a positive attitude and not let a setback get you down, it is also okay to admit that you are disappointed in the results. It is not about saying everything is okay, but about being honest that things are not okay.

The third mindset to avoid is giving yourself negative statements that self-sabotage. It is about waking up and putting on that positive frame of mind that says, even if things didn't work out the way you planned yesterday, you still give yourself positive messages. If you continue to self-sabotage, you are going to develop an attitude of fear, and avoid risks. The growth mindset is based on taking risks to grow, and moving forward without a doom and gloom attitude.

All of us have worked on a team with two kinds of people. There is one that comes to a debriefing of a project, with nothing but doom and gloom to offer about the experience. Then there is the individual who immediately goes to the fact that it wasn't all bad, and focuses on what worked before acknowledging what didn't, and works on potential solutions for next time.

These two people are not going to see eye to eye because they don't have the same mindset. Of the two, which do you think is more likely to grow and thrive professionally? It is easy to see that growth happens when you acknowledge what was done well, what needs to improve, and actively work to improve it.

| Building Grit – The Resilience Factor |

One of the most valuable things I learned is that regardless of the situation I faced, I had the ability to adapt in order to survive it. When I was traveling and living in countries where I didn't speak the language, I adapted and used sign language or miming to communicate. There were frustrations, such as not knowing the names of things, and feeling that I wasn't independent, or being unable to cook the food I was used to because the ingredients were not available in the country that I was living in. I was living in places where there was nothing familiar about my surroundings. The circumstances and experiences taught me both grit and resilience.

What is grit? What is resilience?

To me, grit is your determination to do something, no matter what. I was determined to build a name for myself with my company, as I started it in 2016, and there was nothing that I was going to allow to stop me. No matter what happened, I was not going back to what wasn't growing me, as a person and in my career. I was determined to make it as an entrepreneur. That determination stemmed from my passion in my beliefs, goals, and dreams.

Resilience, on the other hand, is when you face tough moments where you failed. It is the moments when you get up, dust yourself off, and try again. It is really about your mindset. Resilience is about moving forward in a positive way after something has held you back. It really does involve your tenacity. There are a couple of things that it is built on.

The first is your belief in yourself, and the second is how others believe in you. The primary focus is what you believe about yourself, and whether your beliefs and values are in alignment with what is happening around you.

- Do you need to change your environment?
- How connected are you with your own feelings and what is happening around you socially?
- What are the things that you do to keep going with a positive mindset?

These are the things that help you build your personal resilience. Even when you are not doing well, the language you use as part of your self-talk is very impactful. Part of being brave and resilient is to surround yourself with individuals who have the same positive mindset. It can serve to support and inspire you when you feel negatively about a given situation or circumstance.

When you have positive people rallying around you, then you are going to be able to get through whatever you are dealing with. On the other hand, being around negative people is going to drag you down. Developing grit and persistence requires support and positivity throughout your environment.

I admit to having a more rigid thinking pattern, a gift from my rigid background growing up. Perhaps you have recognized an inflexibility in your thinking, or see how you are prone to negative self-talk. Now you might be recognizing a need to change. I had a similar period in my life, when my inflexibility or rigid thinking began to hold me back.

What made me realize that I had to adopt a more flexible pattern of thinking was when I recognized that you could come to the same conclusion using different paths.

We are lucky to have freedom of choice, and multiple solutions are out there. Being adaptable and flexible can make it easier for you when dealing with those who have a different mindset or way of approaching things. Adaptability can also help you to be tenacious in the face of a variety of circumstances. I was personally challenged by the idea of adaptability, but it was here that I was able to grow after putting in the work.

Part of my journey was recognizing the importance of smaller, attainable goals that were in alignment with my beliefs and values. The big goal can often seem to be still out of reach, but those smaller goals can be just what we need in order to keep pushing forward.

One of the blessings of being on my own for the past three years is how much more time I have to be introspective, reflective, and meditative. Part of that journey has involved allowing myself to quiet and listen to my inner voice more carefully. Are you making time to be quiet and listen?

Resilience, grit, and tenacity are not things that just happen overnight. You have to build them, work at it, and give yourself the mental conditioning to get through your challenges. When you do this, you will have such an amazing ability to recover from setbacks that might be debilitating to others. It could be a setback in a relationship, a physical issue, or professional challenges. They all could become roadblocks if you do not have the ability to look at that situation as a growth moment.

| Overcoming the Failure Mentality |

One of the things that is important to do in this process is to change how you look at failure. No matter how good your goals are or how hard you work toward them, failure is something that we will all have to go through. There are going to be moments when you don't do something that you need to, or circumstances shift, and you fail.

I just spoke in the last point about grit and how that can help you to never give up, even when faced with failure. Get reflective, and identify all the valuable lessons that you can take away from that experience. If you don't risk anything, then you are not going to gain anything. Failure is necessary for success.

When you fail and then are successful, you can be proud of the fact that you soldiered through that. Professionally, that soldiering through could mean getting up for work on Monday morning, with a smile on your face, after getting a bad review on Friday. Whatever it is, we have all been in the position of failing and then being successful after we learn and grow.

I have also found that most of the time, failure has impactfully changed me in some way. Over the years, I have developed the mental ability to bounce back from any roadblock or hindrance, because I have gone through multiple challenges. Each time I have dealt with a challenge, it helped me to build confidence, to not be so thin-skinned, and to be more patient. Perhaps you faced the frustration of failure, and felt hopeless, crying at the situation. Recognize that those tears are not going to change what has happened. Looking at failure differently allowed me to transform my thinking, shifting my emotional response from tears of frustration to figuring out my next move or the different options available. I was able to not fear failure, and that has changed me in a positive way.

Here is a simple way to illustrate what I mean. Babies start walking and, along the way, they fall. It becomes a cycle of getting up and falling over and over again. If on the fifth time, they decided not to get up, then that baby would take longer to learn how to walk. The falling part of that baby's growth is when they take two or three steps before they start running. To get to that point, they had to fall.

If you never have the courage to try in the first place, then you are going to convince yourself that you are not capable, and that is when you truly fail. Your self-talk can change how you interpret a situation, for good or bad.

| Using Failure to Fuel Creativity |

How do you change something negative into something positive, as a creative person? I can honestly say that no scientist created their brilliant work because they did it right the first time. They likely did multiple experiments, failed miserably, and may have been put into the position of being a weird member of the family until they succeeded. Then everyone wanted to be their friend and admit that they knew them.

Any person who is a creator or entrepreneur, they have done it because they built their creativity from the things that they didn't do well.

I once heard the story of a village man who wanted to create an affordable sanitary napkin for the women in smaller communities that didn't have access to these items. Most of the women were using clothes, which they washed or simply buried once they were done. His idea was to create something using cheap cotton cloth. He gave samples to women and then asked for them to be returned in order to access their performance. The people around him thought he was nuts. It got so bad that his family ostracized him, his wife divorced him, and he became a pariah in his own community. Eventually, he went on to create a machine that produced sanitary napkins at a reduced rate. Then he trained poor village women on how to use the machine, giving them a means to produce an income. Their pads were sold to an NGO, who gave them to those in need at a significantly reduced rate. He went on to be a TED-X speaker, and a film about his life was created.

If he had gotten stuck on the negativity surrounding his vision, then he would have never had the courage to accomplish what he did. It would have been easy to succumb to the pressure, but he used that negativity to fuel his creativity. Anyone that wants to do something creative, must break free from the social expectations or norms.

Having an innovative and fresh perspective can help you to create something that is useful to the world. Still, that would never happen if you are afraid to step out and try because of the opinions of others.

Being creative, innovative, and thinking outside of the box can lead to some alienation. You should use that alienation to your advantage. Eventually, you will find people to help champion your cause. Then you will be able to make sure that whatever you are doing is in line with your ultimate vision, your goals, and where you want to go.

There are things that can hold you back from being creative. Perhaps you have been told that you don't have any good ideas. When and where you say something, as well as the manner in which you say it, and the audience, can impact how your idea is received. Being creative and innovative is highly required in today's professional world. There are still fields and industries where creativity and innovation are not accepted. Still, if it is worth the effort, then you will find a way to get your idea across that will allow it to be received more positively.

There is also the fear of the unknown, because you really don't know how your idea could be received. Keeping silent means that you don't have to hear the dreaded word, "no." I encourage you to take that chance and make a leap of faith.

The other aspect is that when you are creating, it might not be as logical or as structured as the final project is. When you go through the creative process, you need a flexible mindset to recognize when a brilliant idea needs a lot of tweaking. It is very important to utilize brainstorming, which will give you the ability to weed out the best and most doable ideas. But that process can't happen if you do not allow yourself to bring those ideas forward without fear of judgement or the fear that it will sound illogical.

The fear of judgment can often keep us from speaking up. There is a list of people in our lives that we fear will criticize us or the ideas that we are putting forward. A painter doesn't create his works because he is waiting to hear what other people have to say. That painter creates because there is something within their soul that they want to share.

If your ideas are not being well received in the current arena, then consider changing it. You might start a blog, or branch out into different creative outlets to get across your ideas. A large part of this process involves believing in yourself and the creative ideas that you are bringing out. When you do that, then others will start to find value in you.

A creative mindset is powerful. I feel like I am on fire. Once I start thinking outside of the box, my mind shifts into a mode of constant improvement and adjustment. I am always asking how I can do it better or where I can tweak it to improve. How can I get to where I need to go?

Not a day goes by where I am not using or fueling myself through my creativity. That creativity has helped to develop my analytical and structured side. Both sides of my personality are being used in a more effective way. I feel more fulfilled as well.

| Build the Right Environment to Fuel Your Attitude |

Your winning attitude ties back to how you view yourself and how you talk to yourself. Do you fuel up with positive statements, or break yourself down with negative ones? How we talk to ourselves is a key indicator of how resilient and courageous we are on the road to fulfilling our dreams.

CHAPTER 6 – Making Failures Your Success

I have always said that how you view what is happening in your life is going to determine where you go in your life. Having an attitude of success and belief in yourself will reflect in a number of ways. In Chapter 1, I talked about changing how you talk to yourself in order to bring about changes in your thought process and how you behave. There is a reason why we gravitate toward our positive friends. Every time you are around them, you feel better, more at peace, and more positive. They can serve to encourage you or give you the necessary nudge to get you moving. That can really make a big difference when you are dealing with failure.

It is very easy to determine how well or successful you are based on who you surround yourself with. Get rid of the energy vampires and the negative energy they project. Being around those who always want to argue and bring negativity into the discussion, ends up draining you. After spending time with them, even small hurdles can feel overwhelming. Those interactions can be emotionally draining. A winning attitude means surrounding yourself with people that have the same attitude.

Another way that I keep my positive mindset is by not waking up and filling my head with negative news. It might be challenging at first to turn off the morning news, avoiding those news alerts on your phone, and putting down the morning paper. In the end, it will be worth it, because your mind will not be bathing in negativity as you start your day.

My radio show on the weekends has news items, but I have purposefully started the show with a positive or empowering item, to put positivity out there first. It is because the news is often full of who had died, who had been murdered, who committed a crime, or divisive politics. There is always a negative frame around it. Surrounding myself with positive thoughts, positive people, positive reminders, and positive affirmations is how I maintain my winning attitude—and you can do the same!

Key Takeaways:

- Shift your mindset away from viewing yourself as a failure, and see it as a chance to learn and grow.
- Use failure to fuel your creativity and out-of-the-box thinking.
- Focus on the positive, and avoid falling into a loop of negativity.
- Avoid energy vampires, and surround yourself with those who have the same winning attitude.

There is much of your brand that is based on your mindset, your energy, and your surroundings. Now let's take everything that you have built and put it to good use in creating your badass social media strategy.

PRO TIP

anniejkoshy.com

GET SOCIAL

"To market effectively using social media platforms, you need to identify and know your audience to build your social media presence."

ANNIE KOSHY - AUTHOR
HOW TO BE YOUR BADASS SELF
A Guide to Using Your Inner Energy for Brand Success

CHAPTER 7
BUILD BRAND AWARENESS – GET SOCIAL

| **Chapter 7 -** Build Brand Awareness – Get Social |

Much of social media is about understanding many of the principles of branding, and utilizing them to your advantage. I constantly point out, to the clients I coach, that connecting through social media is best done when you are authentic, allowing people to see who you really are, warts and all. Building your authenticity often starts with building credibility.

I started with Facebook in 2008, and initially saw it as a social platform to connect with family and friends who lived far away. It didn't seem to have a place in my work life until I started seeing people posting about their professional careers and businesses.

Social media has evolved from being purely social to a means of communication with your target market. It is a platform to start purposeful conversations, one that can be very significant for thought leaders. There are different aspects of social media that I learned to harness in more effective ways, which impacted the way I was marketing my brand. I began the initial contact with individuals on social media, based on already having a personal or professional connection to them.

Then it began to evolve because I started to realize that the content related to my brand was not really resonating with my family. That was when I started to realize that I needed targeted pages and audiences for the different aspects of what I was doing to brand myself on social media. These targeted pages lent credibility to the interactions that I wanted to cultivate for my brand.

| **Using Social Media to Gain Credibility** |

To build credibility, you need to have conversations and interactions that make you approachable. Your audience will find that you are more relatable that way.

If you are a comedian, then you use humor. If you are an event coordinator, then you are energetically talking about your events. Initially, this was one of the ways that I built credibility, letting people know there was an actual human behind the keyboard. Even before I started marketing to targeted audiences, I worked on building credibility.

The second aspect was to build content with a message that focused on the audience I was trying to target. The goal was to give them something that captured their attention and helped them to relate to me and my brand.

The third aspect involved responding to people, acknowledging their presence on my page. If I put something out and they wrote a comment on that post, then I made an effort to respond. If I didn't respond, then people would stop wanting to interact with me. Many people, as they get busier, don't spend time responding to their social media. However, if you are trying to build your brand using social media, responding in a timely manner to the comments, on whatever platform you are using, is essential to indicate whether your brand or organization is authentic and interested in building relationships.

Being trustworthy means responding to those who participate in the discussions you start. I have seen thought leaders pose a question, and yet when people respond to that question, there are no replies to their comments. At that point, they are not being courteous, and are burning bridges with their target audience. Building strong relationships with your audience and clients is based on their perception of you and your organization. Their perceptions determine whether they believe you are credible.

| Posting Guidelines for Brand Development |

Make it very clear on your page or website what your brand mission is and what you are trying to do. Essentially, here is where you are sharing the vision for your brand. If you look at my website, my photo, title, and name is there, but I also have been specific about giving voice to the voiceless, through thought leadership, media, and art. That is my tagline, and when you land on my page, it is immediately clear what my brand is trying to do.

When all the other things are listed on my website and on Facebook, each page clearly outlines what aspect of my business it is focused on, including information about what it is and when it started. The goal is to create a foundation for people to understand who I am and what each aspect of my brand is all about.

When you write for your brand, think about the tone you use and the overall voice. People can tell when you are writing in a voice that is not authentic to you and your brand. This voice needs to reflect you as a person, or your brand's mission and vision. Your brand identity is related to even the simplest details, such as the color, font, and letter size. On social media, your voice is made up of all these parts.

There are certain reasons why financial organizations use specific colors in their marketing strategy to build credibility with their audience, and that extends to the photos used in their media and marketing.

Another aspect of your social media platform has to involve your logo. Where it is placed, the size of it, how it is used, and more, are all part of the consistency of your brand, regardless of the platform. Choose a specific color palette, and then stick with it across the various platforms. If you are using red, then it should be a specific shade as part of that color palette. Understand what your logo and those colors will look like in different formats, from print to the web, and choose your color palette to be compatible across those platforms.

Let's be clear; there are going to be differences in how your logo looks on a mobile device compared to a desktop across these different platforms. Make sure to check if your colors, fonts, photos, art, and other aspects of your logo are coming across clean and clear.

Is your logo going to use images or photos? I have a specific style of photography that I use as part of my logo for my imagery and branding. Part of your social media efforts involves determining the images and photos that align with your brand and its message. Those stylistic methods are essential to create as part of your brand.

Consistency involves having the same message in your digital media and print media with tweaks to reflect the unique aspects of each platform. A strong logo is going to highlight your colors and your business. However, you may need to adjust size and color shades slightly, giving you the ability to apply consistency in your branding across multiple platforms.

Creating a stylistic guide for your brand, which outlines how your brand should be presented on each platform, is a must. When your marketing team has this guide, then changes can go much smoother. You will have less fear of inconsistency, simply because they can pick up that guide and follow it. Here are just a few of the areas your stylistic guide should cover:

- Banners/Signs
- Facebook posts
- Website
- Letterhead
- Business cards
- Print advertising
- Thumbnails for YouTube videos

As they all come together in the same style, that sets the tone for your brand across all your media and marketing platforms.

| Be Seen to Be Heard |

You cannot develop a brand by hiding behind a curtain. Like the Wizard, eventually the curtain will be pulled, and who you are will be revealed. In order to develop your brand and connect with others, you have to get out there and be seen, talking to others and building a network. The process of talking about your brand also helps to build its brand identity. Why is that so important?

Once this process begins, your company will need someone to be the face of the brand, associating a human element with it. Companies are hyper aware of who is associated with their brands because they recognize the emotional connection it can create. Using celebrities and sports figures can be appealing, but many companies have had to disassociate themselves with these individuals for a variety of reasons, including actions that are not in line with the company's vision. Tiger Woods is a good example. As his personal life imploded a few years back, brands began to drop him as one of their representatives. His personal issues being so public meant that it reflected badly on their brands and their messaging. There are numerous examples of athletes losing multi-million-dollar sponsors because they have fallen from grace. The people chosen to be your face are contributing to building the credibility of your brand, which is why brands make changes when those two things no longer align.

Consider hiring a recruiter that understands the culture of your organization, to bring on people to your team that enhance and build onto that culture. It is not just about your product and services, but establishing a face and credibility over time to build trust and rapport. You can reach out to me on my website, or on one of my social media pages, if you are an organization needing assistance with recruiting new staff or downsizing your existing team. If you are an individual and require assistance in job strategizing or in updating your professional presence, then reach out to my team. We will put you in touch with the right folks who will lend a hand.

Personally, I tend to question the reliability of an organization that has a skeleton website, with no pictures of their team, and just a barebones description of their company. There are three aspects that play a part, including having a face, building trust with a message that people understand, and making it clear what your brand is offering, while keeping your industry in mind. Even the photos of your team need to reflect your brand mission. If you have an artsy company, for example, then the photos should reflect that, not be boring generic images. People might not want to hire you, simply because the personality and creativity of your brand isn't coming through. Now, a bank, on the other hand, would probably avoid those more artistic images, because individuals might not take them seriously as a financial institution.

As part of this process, consider doing a SWAT analysis regarding your branding and messaging. After marketing campaigns, for instance, these analyses helped us determine what the strengths and weaknesses of a campaign were.

Doing one for your brand identifies its strengths and weaknesses, where you can grow, and what needs to change immediately. This process is essential as you build your brand. When you market yourself at a different level, then your brand can stand out from the crowd. Part of your journey will involve keeping abreast of the latest industry trends to stay one step ahead of your competition. Once you start a new business or branding process, gauge whether what you have been putting out there is working for you. Being flexible to change and adapting it according to what you are doing, is important. While your overall theme may be consistent across platforms, specific events or advertising may need to be tweaked to reflect a different tagline. This approach allows for more targeted marketing related to specific events.

People love stories, and those stories help people to emotionally connect to your brand. It builds your personality with your audience, allowing them to connect with you as a human, and build rapport and trust.

| Be Your Brand Ambassador |

What is a brand ambassador? It is a representative for your team, someone in your company, amongst your employees or volunteers. Being a brand ambassador is about creating the right face-to-face interactions for your company, with clients and the outside world. They represent the human element of your brand.

If you are running an organization with a wide range of employees, then everyone needs to know that they are now brand ambassadors, even when they leave the company's physical structure. This is why many organizations are upset by social media posts that reflect badly on them. If you are an employee and list your connection with your employer, and then you go out and post photos of a wild night of partying, then you could be seen as distracting from that brand identity. Our world has evolved to where social media is an open platform, where companies market their worth but can also blur the line between employees' personal and professional lives.

When you are associating with, work with, or are hired by a brand, then you are a brand ambassador. If I am bringing someone to assist me with one of my events, then they are not there to promote their work; they are representing my brand. There are certain things that you need to groom your team on to make sure that their actions reflect your brand message.

When you put out material on social media platforms, your brand ambassadors will put that content out across social media platforms, and then you can measure the analytics to see how it is received and shared. As brand ambassadors, they also can assist with demonstrations of your products at trade shows or other industry events. Word of mouth is also another aspect of the work of a brand ambassador, as they share their experiences and the benefits of your brand.

Communication with your brand ambassadors is also key to successful events. How? Through that communication, I have made sure they have everything necessary to be successful.

Before the event, I send out an email, defining the event, what is part of the set-up and breakdown, as well as assigning roles. Plus, I define their wardrobe, which is meant to be comfortable enough for them to do their job, while being as unobtrusive as possible. Everyone knows exactly what they are doing, as well as how they should look while performing their assignments, and it makes for a seamless experience for my clients. The truth is that for every face in the front, greeting clients, there is also a behind-the-scenes team that is also serving to create an amazing brand experience. As brand ambassadors, my whole team is creating the experience I had envisioned, and boosting the reputation of my company in the process.

How have I asked people to be brand ambassadors online? I constantly am building my content, and then my marketing team puts it out online. When I have an event, I always have co-hosts, who are then able to share and invite others to that event. Thus, the reach of that event increases. When I post on Instagram, I share it across all my related platforms. People who attend my events are asked to give reviews about the event itself or any of the services that my team has provided. Reviews, on such platforms as Google and Yelp, are critical to building credibility online, and can help future clients learn what you and your brand are like.

| Developing Your Bank of Content |

Throughout these chapters, you have clearly seen the need for quality content. Now the question is how to create that content in a way that positively impacts the brand.

Look at the beginning of each chapter; there is an image that I created. That means I approved the font, how the colours were used, the layout, and the placement of these images within the text itself.

The quote in these images comes from the book's material. These are aspects that I have built purposefully to be reflective of my brand. The point is to build content that positively reflects your messaging, be it through signs, posts, emails, blogs, vlogs, or video content.

The point of all of this is to effectively market yourself using social media platforms and including your content. Identify who your audience is, and build a social media presence that speaks to that audience. When I was building my bank of content, it was reflective of my colours, my branding, and what I wanted my audience to know about me and my company. I also tailored my content to fit the platform that it was showcased on, be it Facebook, Instagram, or another social media network. It doesn't make sense to create content that won't fit the frame of that platform.

Having a solid social media marketing strategy is also important in guiding your content creation.

- What are you planning on creating?
- What platforms are you planning on using?
- Are you going to be balancing it with live content, such as videos or vlogs?
- Will you be producing written blogs?
- Do you have events that are happening?
- Do you have targeted public service announcements or other tidbits of information that you want to share?
- Do you have thought leaders or mentors, whose thoughts and ideas you want to put out because they inspire or motivate you?
- When are you going to be marketing your brand and its content?

I am constantly building content, and some of the content that I build for one platform may be effective or a good fit for another platform. You may create a 1-minute ad for YouTube that you could repurpose into a 30-second ad for Facebook, and that could be repurposed again into a 15-second ad for Instagram.

One piece of content has multiple uses across several platforms. This process will also help with consistency across all your brand's platforms.

Avoid doing things just because someone else is doing them. Focus on content that works for your brand and messaging. Even if your competition is doing something that your company really doesn't do, steer clear of knee jerk responses that have you making the same thing. Just because you are both in the same sector or industry, doesn't mean that you have to follow them in terms of content. Be trendy on your own, and stay true to your brand, both on social media and offline.

As you measure the effectiveness of your content, be honest with yourself in gauging how your brand is doing. This honesty will help you to make necessary adjustments. If something is not going the way it should, access it and try again. Avoid putting up a question to engage your audience that is not reflective of your content. Think about why you are asking that question.

- Is the question serving as a guide for the type of content you want to provide based on the feedback you are receiving?
- Where is your content going, and why are you creating it?

Understanding why is important to knowing what you are going to create in terms of content. Your brand core value has to be communicated in all the content that you create, right from the get-go.

Determine your budget, broken down by quarters, half yearly, or annually, and how you want to spread it out across your chosen platforms. This will give you an idea of how much money you will need to spend for various campaigns and content creation. I have been very focused on the type of clientele that I want to build for my brand, so I tailor my content to reflect the demographics I am trying to reach, as well as focus on the platforms they frequent.

| Targeted Posting |

As I build an audience, I learn when they are going to be online, and I tailor the timing and content of my posts to reflect that. For instance, a post regarding business is not likely to get much traction on Friday evening. Additionally, if you are posting anything to a group, then you need to be aware of whether you are meeting their guidelines. If you are posting appropriately, then you are more likely to be favorably received by that audience.

One of my biggest pet peeves is tagging. Please do not tag people who are not directly related to the content that you are posting, especially if you have not asked their permission. I see a lot of people who do not understand the social etiquette related to social media marketing. Personally, it drives me crazy to be tagged on posts that I have no connection to as a social media marketer. . I am hired to use my branding platform on social media, so to be tagged without hiring my services is frustrating. Knowing who and what to tag, as well as asking permission to tag, is very important. There are ways to do that without risking relationships or diminishing the reputation of your brand.

Another important aspect is not to flood your audience with posts and content. Doing so could lead to your being blocked or unfollowed, which is counter to your goals of using social media in the first place.

A lot of people think that just because you have access to your friends' list of friends on a social media platform, they are now fair game to make connections with. As social media becomes a professional, as well as personal platform, it is important to build connections in a way that reflects well on you and your brand. Just because a friend has a connection with someone who is at a higher vibration or higher income, does not mean that you can just reach out, connect with them, and then start to market to them. Building a network takes time and effort.

It is important to get training about social media etiquette. Not everyone in your friends' circles are going to appreciate having you marketing to their circles. Be careful about marketing to the connections of your connections, because it can appear that you are using a rival's social media network to build your own. Without etiquette, it becomes a free-for-all that can be damaging to your brand.

Instead, focus on growing your content and building connections with thought leaders. Those interactions can build your credibility with your target audience, and create long-term growth.

Key Takeaways:
- Create engaging content based on your brand and target audience.
- When engaging with your target audience, participation is key to keeping their interest and increasing your reputation of reliability and credibility.
- Shape content to fit multiple platforms, allowing you to engage with your target audience in various interactions.
- Practice social media etiquette to avoid damaging your brand.

With all the content you are creating, and the brand reputation that you are building, it is critical to be consistent across all types of marketing, not just social media. Let's talk about how it all combines to create your image, as well as the power of imagery in all aspects of your brand messaging.

anniejkoshy.com

IMAGES ARE YOUR DIGITAL CARD

"Don't underestimate the power of a good photograph.

Brand yourself before someone else brands you!"

ANNIE KOSHY - AUTHOR
HOW TO BE YOUR BADASS SELF
A Guide to Using Your Inner Energy for Brand Success

CHAPTER 8
YOUR PICTURE IS YOUR CALLING CARD

_____

| **Chapter 8 -** Your Picture Is Your Calling Card |

The saying is true: "Image is everything!" However, an image is not just the pictures you post or the outfits you wear to industry events. It involves all the aspects of your branding. If you don't take control of your image, then someone else will define it for you, and their perceptions and judgements might not be in your favor.

For example, auditions are one place where image is critical. You will have people show up, looking sloppy, without headshots, or even a resume. They are perceived as underachievers, not serious, and unlikely to produce. Can you imagine being cut before you say a word? It happens more than people realize, simply because they didn't create the right image and then moved forward with it.

I have talked about my brand colours several times, and how it wraps into your brand message. Today, I have a uniform of my colours, which I wear consistently. Instead of allowing trends to define my image, I have chosen to brand myself.

Even when it comes to social media, you can create the wrong image if you aren't careful. Your posts might be all over the place, and people draw the wrong conclusions about who you are and what you are about, as a result. Branding yourself helps to reiterate what your story is about and gets your message across. Whatever outfacing communication you may have, the entire package has to properly reflect your image.

| **Branding Your Look** |

I spoke in the last chapter about how important it is to be personable for your clients, including the perceptions that your overall image gives. You need to have a defined look that ties to your brand and goals.

If you are planning on heading your own company, or are still working for someone else and looking to move up into a senior position, then along with doing quality work, you need to dress the part.

To be the boss, dress like the boss. If your corporate culture is professional dress, then do that in a way that makes you stand out, without standing apart in a way that leaves people confused. There may be days, such as Friday, where the dress code is relaxed or more chill. This is your opportunity to bring in something related to your own personal brand, allowing you to stand out in a unique way. Folks can show up in jeans and a t-shirt, but even that can be unique. There are a variety of styles and colours that you can use to create your brand. Steve Jobs, for instance, always showed up in a black t-shirt or turtleneck. That was his go-to look, and everyone recognized that he dressed that way.

It doesn't matter if you are going to the office, a more artistic space, or even the gym—depending on your job, then you are representing your brand. For instance, if you are a personal trainer, there might be a unique style that you wear into the gym that becomes associated with you and your brand.

This process is not about a uniform but creating a personal look as part of an overall package regarding how you want people to look at you in terms of your brand and persona.

Having said that, there are some folks who will take it to the other extreme. They are too busy, and the result is that they end up looking too much for the situation. The style guide I would suggest here, to make yourself unique, is to choose one bold piece or color that becomes your branding look. To choose that statement piece, consider:

- What is your focus?
- What are you trying to do with your branded self?

Having a statement piece as part of your look, will help you stand out in people's memories, but it is also important to be genuine. Create your own niche, and don't copy someone else. Focus on your own strengths as you create your niche, and that is what you will become known for within your environment.

My personal brand is woven into all the different hats that I wear professionally and personally, as well as throughout my website, social media, and communication. Make your image personable and genuine to make the greatest branding impact.

| Stand Out to Stand Apart |

One of the first things that makes me stand out when I walk into a room is my confidence. I walk into the room with my head held high, shaking hands with confidence, speaking with confidence, and even sitting erect. When someone walks into a room and they appear unkempt or slouching, then it has a huge impact on the impression that they make. Style is very important, depending on the work that you are doing. Projecting that style into your work is very important. As a model, if I show up on set with wrinkled clothes, then that will give a negative impression.

The impression that you are creating needs to match the message that you are putting out regarding your brand and your look. The confidence comes across with that look, along with your body language and presentation. Some cultures see looking someone directly in the eye as disrespectful, so it is important to be conscious of culture as well. Depending on where you are and your relationship with the subordinates and seniors, you may need to step it up and practice those cultural norms, to make them a natural extension of how you present yourself in those circumstances.

Being culturally sensitive to where you are, what you are presenting, and who you are presenting it to, will help you to make a good impression.

There may be times when you come across a project and you don't yet have the skills, but you want to do it. My first rule of thumb for growth is to get uncomfortable, and that starts by taking on these big projects where you might not be as sure of yourself. Take it on, and learn as you do it. Believe in yourself and your ability to grow and learn. You can build on your grit and perseverance. Taking on those initiatives also speaks well of you, and has a positive impact on your image. If you have these things coming up, and they are a bit out of your comfort zone, then be open to taking it on anyway. By doing that, you build on your foundation and accept a challenge. It says two things about you and your brand. One, it speaks volumes about you as a person and your ability to take the initiative. Two, it speaks to your need and plan of continual growth. You can only grow if you are challenging yourself.

After an event, when you are debriefing with your team, take the opportunity to let your voice be heard. One of the tools to do so was discussed in the last chapter, known as a SWOT analysis.

This is the chance to access what went well and where we could have done better, as well as where we need to change. Part of that process involves giving your perspective and letting your voice be heard. Remember, you are on the team for your expertise. Speaking out regarding the event is going to be very important and a part of your professional image.

Standing out showcases your tenacity. You may have joined a company, and during that first quarter, you might not have yet made an impression. Do not let that deter you. Focus on your message and what you are trying to accomplish, as well as how and when your voice is being consistently heard.

One of the things that I do when meeting a new client is to arm myself with information. I know everything about that client by looking through their website, reading about them, and really doing my homework. When I am on the air and talking about a potential guest, I will have already set up a meeting with that guest to talk with them before I do the live interview.

I go through their background and look at their work in comparison to others in their industry, formulating my questions based on industry standards, while also targeting them specifically.

Another aspect of my live interviews is to listen very carefully to the responses. It is one thing to come across strong and confident as an interviewer, but I would be putting off my listeners and guests if I didn't pay attention to what they were saying.

Now let's take that out to a meeting. If I am not listening to what you have to say, then it will be hard for me to give feedback based on that later on, or to be engaged in the process. If you are steamrolling everyone's ideas because you are not listening to what is being said, and you are not flexible enough to adapt your ideas based on what has already been said, then you are going to stand out for the wrong reasons.

Listening and adapting are critical to being part of a team, but at the same time, you can build that team in a positive way. When someone gives feedback and you acknowledge that, it makes them feel that they have been heard, and it gives you the chance to express your own ideas. How you work in a group is built on whether you can do that.

Your ability to be a leader is going to depend on whether you can hear what others say and build on that feedback. Going into any meeting, it is key to have an agenda. It is one of the ways that you can hone your ability to be specific and task-oriented. This allows you to have a clear understanding of the expectations of the meetings and what needs to be accomplished.

Getting specifics helps to keep things in alignment in several ways. The first is in terms of time constraints. The second is your acknowledgement and respect for the members of your team that need to prepare items for the meeting by giving them the time to do so. Those specifics can also include providing background information about the individuals or companies, especially if the meeting is meant to be an introductory one. Thus, you are introducing them on an equal playing field, while also building relationships.

These are things that I have learned help to build bridges between people, and get them on the same platform in my line of work. If you look at your goals and what you are doing to achieve them, then these are some key aspects of standing out to stand apart from your competitors. It is how you do business and engage your clients.

| Your Engaging Smile |

One of the things that people often comment on when they first meet me is my smile, which is a blessing. It is engaging and reaches out from my eyes. My smile tells right away how I am feeling. There are different types of smiles, and they are an important part of your communication. Smiles are an important way to engage your audience and help you come across as friendly and approachable. Someone who doesn't smile may be a great individual with an engaging personality, and they may be highly educated, but they come across as dower and unapproachable. No one really wants to be around them. On the other hand, a smile can win someone over before you say a word. With that in mind, let's look at the variety of ways that you can put your smile to good use.

There are a variety of smiles that we can focus on. I have come across people who have a lack of trustworthiness, simply by the way that they smile and shake hands.

You might have also seen the smile where it almost seems as if they have a stomachache. The smile just doesn't quite reach their eyes. They are pretending to be happy. People who smile for the camera can turn it on, but it is not very believable. If your image is being used and you have one of those fake smiles on, then your image could end up being a turn off.

One of the things you have to look at is how you are smiling. That may mean standing in front of the mirror and practicing your smile. This process might not be easy for you. Some people are very uncomfortable with smiling. If they are uncomfortable and trying to smile, that uncomfortable feeling is going to shine through their smile. For example, if you are not comfortable having your picture taken, and you are wearing a suit, with a photographer standing in front of you to take a picture for your social media profile, you might smile, but those who know you will immediately be able to tell, from that image, that you are uncomfortable.

The other way that you know someone is smiling uncomfortably can happen when you are in a group, and someone says something that is off-colour. They may laugh, but their laugh and smile reflect that they are uncomfortable but do not want to rock the boat with the whole group.

Then you have body language that is used in a way to send a message of seduction. This is a different form of smile, but not appropriate in a corporate setting or as you are building business connections. We all have different aspects of our personalities, and different smiles to go with them. Which one are you using as part of your image as your company's brand ambassador? The difference between your smiles is the look in your eyes and how well the photograph reflects that.

| The Importance of a Professional Photo |

Having an engaging smile is just one part of your brand. A picture tells the story of your personal brand, and if you want to come across as a credible, reliable, and trustworthy person, then having a photo that is murky will not help you get that message across.

The photo needs to reflect what you want to say, as well as the image that you have as a person. Professional photographers can be a great way to capture what you want, recognizing how all the environmental aspects play into creating a great image.

As I mentioned in the section, Standing Out to Stand Apart, you need to incorporate your bold colour or action piece, but make sure that it is not overpowering within the photo. All of those elements need to be in alignment with your messaging.

The photos and images you use will start to build the legacy of your brand. As your brand grows, people will be looking at the evolution of you as an individual, and the evolution of your brand.

Why are photos important in your brand, on your social media feed, and how you present yourself? Images are much more than a record of you as a person. They are a record of different aspects of your business as well. For my own website, the images that I have used to relay or convey text have been purposely put there. I do not use stock imagery. As much as possible, I try to use the authentic image that I have created to represent my brand. It speaks about my passion for photography, as well as my passion to engage the audience authentically as part of the relationship that I have built in my business practice. The photos are representative of my clients or the work that I have done. My photographs, because I do artography, represent my brand as an artist, combined with my photography. It is a combination of this that creates my own unique art form and messaging.

I have not sent out my website and social media content for others to create. I am a hands-on social media entrepreneur, who has built my brand and who curates content based on the specific aspects of my brand. It is very complex to have photography for your website that is in line with all the aspects of your brand, including your colours, messaging, and platform. But taking the time to do that ties it all together.

Yes, it took me a long time to build it, and the process was a lot of ongoing work, but it was worth it. The reality is that this will be an ongoing process. Don't think that at some point you will reach the end and it is done. It is a constantly evolving thing, and to keep your brand fresh and moving forward, you need to constantly be looking at your imagery and content to evolve it, as your brand messaging changes over time.

One of the most important reasons to have those professionally taken photos on your social media is that it really grabs the attention of your audience, particularly those who might end up being potential clients. Using photos is part of the process of building an emotional connection with your audience. There is a reason that National Geographic uses specific iconic pictures on their covers. It grabs attention and is the hook to get people to pick up that book and open it up to check out the contents. This process extends to fashion magazines and tabloid news.

When you are using a specific visual for social media or on your website, the goal should be to grab your audience in a predetermined way. For instance, the font and image used for the biopic on my life was specific in terms of the colouring and lighting.

A photo is a very powerful way to engage your audience, and to have a professional photo taken to brand yourself is absolutely key. For those of you who bought this book, please visit my website and get in touch with me for an opportunity to have branded photographs, taken by me, for your website or brand.

| Why Being "Found" is Important |

There are so many businesses that have created a great website or storefront. They have a lot of contact with their clients and think their business is doing well. The truth is that they are not engaging their clients and are not really out there. One of the important things about marketing, and one of the reasons that you really need to do it, is because you are engaging and meeting your clients where they are.

When it comes to marketing, many business owners have underestimated the power of social media, as we discussed in Chapter 7. However, it is one of the best ways to engage with your clients. If you are not active and putting out what you are doing and how your business is developing, then people are not going to know. You have to tell your clients your story, and put out what you are offering.

It is like going to a restaurant or fast food joint. If they didn't have a menu, then you wouldn't know what they are offering or what your options are, even if they give you their options verbally. People want to see it and be able to buy into it based on the image. If you put out information into a new market, but include no pictures with it, then people don't know what it is.

Imagine a restaurant, such as McDonald's, opening up a location in a new market. They might share what they offer, but if they didn't include pictures, then people might be turned off by what they receive when they order. Why? Because they may have expected one thing, and what they received did not match their expectation. Having that image tying what it is, along with the print, helps you to market your content and give an accurate picture of what your customers are going to receive.

If you want to be found, then put out what you want them to find out about you, in a format that is interesting and worth their time.

Social media is definitely a way to engage your clients, but what are you engaging them on? When I put out a post on a social media platform, I look at the analytics. These tell me what posts were engaged with the most, who engaged with that post, and where they engaged with that post. It also helps me to know who clicked on that post from different areas, and breaks down demographics that were engaged. It helps me to determine what worked best, and that analysis helps me to determine how I need to build my brand and where I might need to change it up.

The other part about being found is building your company's reputation by being consistent and maintaining that reputation in relation to your initial messaging. Frequently, I go back to the "about" page on my social media platforms, and I make sure that the content I am putting out relates to that specific page and is relevant to its message. Effective marketing, communication, and branding throughout your social media platforms is one way that you are going to be found. Building up your relationship with your clientele and engaging them, means targeting those who are most likely to be interested in a specific event or offering from your business. This part of my marketing plan is segmentation, which is another aspect of your image, where I am thinking about specific individuals within my clientele, and targeting them with content to match their interests. That helps to build trust and credibility, as well as avoiding spamming my audience.

People come to my page and stay there when I am respectful of the reason that they came to my page in the first place. I use links to give them opportunities to learn about the other aspects of my work; thus, I am co-branding them. That lets them make an informed decision about how they want to get in contact with me. It goes back to consistent communication across my products and content so that it is in alignment with the message of my company and my image as a whole.

One of the key reasons I have been able to build my marketing, increase sales, and bring people to me is through my consistency and co-branding on social media. While people might think that social media is just a social platform, there are others who realize the power of these platforms for business networking. There are several ways to build your income streams through your social media marketing, such as linking up to events that provide income when people buy tickets. Being found on social media allows you to connect and generate revenue from multiple streams.

| Building Trust Through Authenticity |

Business owners used to build trust with their clients when they engaged with them, after meeting them and growing the relationship over time. However, with social media, you are networking and meeting people in a digital forum. They might not necessarily know you or what your business is about, and the ability to build a relationship might be challenged. There can be cases where you have someone referred to you by a third party, or someone who has already done business with you and had a positive experience, or by word of mouth or review on your page. All of these contribute to building trust in your brand and are contributing to how people perceive your brand image.

There are a number of aspects that help you to build your trust and credibility. If you are trying to do so through your social media platforms, then you need to be transparent in your interactions, authentic in your communications, and responsive to your clients.

I have to be my authentic self; so, when people come to me for my professional advice, I give them feedback to help grow them, and not because I think I will gain another business contact or opportunity. People come to me for those authentic interactions because they know they are going to get the truthful answer from me.

As you build your brand and grow what you do, the conversations and interactions that you have, and the feedback relayed on your pages, through reviews, comments, and team feedback, is going to build your authenticity and reliability, which will build up your trust and credibility. It is not just about a photograph. Truly building a brand means recognizing that your image is a composite of your logo, imaging, and content. It is all encompassing.

Key Takeaways:

- Your image is a combination of how you present yourself on multiple platforms, as well as how you present yourself in person.
- If you are looking to grow in your professional career, then examine how you are presenting yourself and what image you are projecting.
- Use professional photos and images to convey the right message about you and your brand.
- Be authentic and consistent to build trust in you and your brand.

Throughout these chapters, every aspect of your brand image has been discussed. Now it is time to delve into your "why," the reason that you are creating this brand in the first place, and discuss how you make your dreams and purpose come true, regardless of where you are in the stream of building your personal brand.

| Notes |

anniejkoshy.com

DREAM BIG, ACHEIVE BIG

"My success began with a dream. I added a dash of hard work, a spoonful of grit, and a whole lot of dedication. It was baked to perfection in the oven called life."

ANNIE KOSHY - AUTHOR
HOW TO BE YOUR BADASS SELF
A Guide to Using Your Inner Energy for Brand Success

CHAPTER 9
DREAM BIG, ACHIEVE BIG

| **Chapter 9** - Dream Big, Achieve Big |

| **Purposeful Existence** |

This chapter is all about why big dreams are important, and why they need to fuel what you are doing. If we were to summarize what we have been discussing, from the first chapter, which focused on your personal purpose, to now, it has been an opportunity to take stock of your successes, natural abilities, and the skills you have acquired or are applying, but also what has been sitting on the back burner that needs to be brought forward.

Taking an inventory of all of this helps you to create a list of your strengths and to identify your passions. Fueling what you do, with passion, is crucial because it will fire you up mentally, physically, and spiritually, in everything that you are doing to further those goals. Passion for what you are doing becomes your energy drink.

Combining play and work, known as plorking, is something that I am happy to say I have been doing for the last several years, and it has been the absolute best thing. The combination of doing what I am passionate about, and what is fulfilling to me as part of my work, has been key. You can do it too, and live as your badass self in all areas of your life!

Another aspect of this process is to be introspective and accepting of yourself as a person. That means accepting what you have been through, your own expectations, and the space that you are in. When you accept who you are and your own purpose, then you will find yourself breathing a sigh of relief. It means you are not focused on living up to others' expectations, but you are accepting of where you are at that moment. The pressure of unrealistic expectations is off, and now you are ready to create the change you want, to live your best badass life!

One of the things that you need to determine before you get to your short and long-term goals, is what might be holding you back.

- What do you need to let go of?
- What has not been fulfilling you?
- What may be detracting from your ultimate goal?

It could be something emotionally, maybe past failures. I encourage you to sit in a meditative mode and get introspective. Listen to what your inner voice has to tell you. Also, take stock and determine the purpose of what you are doing.

If you start to learn to trust your intuition, and take stock of the things that have been holding you back from listening to it, then that will show you what is holding you back from your purposeful existence. You also need to be in tune with what your body is feeling. If you are not getting enough sleep, not exercising or moving, and not eating right, then you are not going to have a healthy mind.

All of these aspects work in conjunction with each other to harness that inner energy of yours. If you are looking for happiness from external things, such as the ideal job, the ideal house, the latest fashions, or making a lot of money, then you are going to be disappointed. In the words of Ralph Waldo Emerson, "The purpose of life is not to be happy. It is to be useful, to feel honor or to be honorable, to be compassionate, to make a difference in other people's lives, and therefore, to feel that you have lived well."

If you feel that you haven't been doing that, and your happiness has come from external sources, then take the time to figure out why you are feeling the way you are, and what you need to get rid of in order to change that.

| Long-Term and Short-Term Goals |

One of the aspects that I have spoken of extensively is taking stock and setting goals. Earlier, I used the example of wanting to become a fitness trainer. If you put a picture of a fitness trainer on your mirror, yet you wake up flabby, overweight, and disillusioned, then you are going to look at that picture and be even less motivated than you were before. If that is your ultimate goal, then that picture might actually turn into a roadblock. To get into that space, you need to define what will help to motivate you, and that involves setting short- and long-term goals.

In order for anything to happen, you need to act. Nothing is going to change without action. To live your purposeful existence, then you need to take action on your dreams, turning them into actionable goals. You put it out into the universe what you want to do, and the universe is going to respond by saying you need to do x, y, and z. If you sit on your behind and don't move, because you decide that someone else is going to do it, or you opt to wait for the perfect circumstances, then it is never going to happen.

You have to take those steps (x, y, and z) for it to occur.

Let's start by defining short- and long-term goals. A short-term goal is something that can be accomplished in a relatively short period of time, such as a week, a month, three months, or six months. It is something that is attainable but is a component of your long-term goals and desires. A long-term goal could take a period of over a year or more for some of us who are unpacking our goals. In my case, I have a definite idea of where I want to be in six months. If I can do what I want to do in six months, rather than a year, then I am going to be able to backward plan from that, designing from the goal and determining where I want to be today. I set my short-term goals on an easier, more attainable scale to reach that long-term, six-month goal.

The short-term goals need to fuel what your long-term goal expectations are. For example, you want to be a doctor or make a substantial career move. In order to achieve that, you need to do specific things. If you are looking for a promotion as your big career move, then you may need to prove yourself to justify receiving it. On the other hand, if you are looking to get that medical degree, you need to go to college and complete specific courses, as well as on-the-job training to gain specific skills.

There are even further goals after that, which include an apprenticeship or more. Perhaps you have the goal of owning a family practice after so many years of practicing medicine. Each long-term goal leads to the next and smaller goals as part of the process along the way.

Begin the goal that is furthest out, and work your way back. In my example about becoming a doctor, that could include outlining where you want to apply for your residency, what college you want to go to, the type of medicine that you want to specialize in, and more.

Start with your vision of where you want to go and what you want to do, and then plan backward from there to build your list of goals to achieve it. Next, it is really important to write that plan and those goals down. A dream or a goal, without being articulated on paper, is just a figment of your imagination, and it will stay that way.

If you want to achieve something or be something, then you need to have a clearly defined set of goals. However, it is not enough just to write these goals down. Have an action plan that will allow you to see success by measuring your progress. Divide your action plan into a timeframe for achieving your short-term goals, which will lead to the successful completion of your long-term aspirations.

Be your own positive affirmation to achieve your goals. When you wake up, inspire yourself by being your own inspiration. Look at what you have already accomplished, and allow it to motivate you to complete what is in front of you.

Start by taking stock of what you can do, what you need to do, and what you can learn to do. If it is in a business, one of the important things to remember is that you can't become a success by yourself. Surround yourself with people that have complimentary skills or skills that you lack. See if they can mentor you or become part of your team. Every successful person is not successful on their own. They have people surrounding them who helped them to get to where they are. Being realistic is such a crucial aspect of determining your goals. Setting goals that are unattainable is actually more damaging to you in the long run.

If you are not good at science, but you want to become a doctor, that might not be realistic. If, on the other hand, you are good at sales, then perhaps you could sell products and services to the medical community. As a result, your goals would focus on learning the tips and tricks, and understanding the products and market, to become the best sales marketer possible.

This makes your goals and the skills you want to acquire realistic, because you are not becoming a doctor, but you are able to be a part of that industry, with the strengths and skills that you do have.

The other aspect of being realistic is having a doable time frame. It is fine to have realistic goals, but if the time frame is out of reach, then those goals become unattainable. For instance, to become a doctor by 23, might be an unreasonable time frame, whereas setting the goal of being a doctor by the time you are 32, is a reasonable and attainable time frame to complete that goal. Being flexible and open minded is important as well.

| Applaud Each Milestone |

As you go through each of your short-term goals, why is applauding those milestones so important? The primary reason I launched my company is that there are plenty of talented people in this industry that are working in silos. For every person that becomes the representation of a brand in public, there is an army of people behind the scenes helping them to get to that spot.

My company was in recognition of all the different components and jobs that make people who are in the arts, media, and entertainment industries successful. We were not applauding each other's success, particularly those that contribute to it.

What about those people who were the event organizers or selling the tickets that made it a successful night? What about the venue organizers themselves that make a space available for an artist to come in, and that artist becomes successful?

When we look at the success for a brand, there are so many critical components that play a part. Accomplishments from these components should be applauded by the collective.

If you are running an entrepreneurship or a small business, or even running a large corporation, it is important to acknowledge and applaud the successes of every cog in the wheel. Without that cog or screw, if you take it out, then your wheel is not going to run as smoothly as you wish it would.

As employers, the more you pour into your employees and elevate them to be successful, the more successful you and your business will be. This is such a crucial aspect for employers to understand. When you pour into your employees, then they will pour back into you. If this basic truth is uncovered, understood, and applied, then it would lead to so much more in terms of employee retention, employee happiness, productivity, and better attitudes and presence.

With your team, if you applaud the milestones, both personally and for your team as a whole, then you are going to be successful overall.

| Utilize the Power of Your Mind |

We do not realize how powerful our mind strength really is. For myself, in my goddess moment of harnessing this power, it is about directing my energy into what my purpose has been. Your mind strength should not be expended randomly, doing it one day but not the next. Be focused, and know who you are as a person to be able to hone in on what it is that you really want to do. Then apply the positive mental attitude to that ultimate purpose. You are in control of every thought that comes into your mind. If you are controlling your thoughts, which allow you to feel a certain way, to do a certain thing, and to create your own existence, then you are harnessing your emotions, your energy, your skills, and your attitude.

There are so many aspects contributing to your thoughts. If you are looking to others for approval and acknowledgement, then you are going to be setting yourself up for unhappiness.

Sometimes if your purpose and goal is not in alignment with what is going on around you, then learning to say no is going to be key. Always surround yourself with people who are going to build you up around your purpose or reasons for the actions you are taking and the choices you are making.

That is not to say that you should surround yourself with specific individuals for selfish reasons. When you surround yourself with like-minded individuals, then you are all working in harmony with each other toward a unified goal, creating a mastermind experience. You end up elevating each other for that success. It is not saying that you are providing services free of cost, but that each of you within this group will receive some fulfillment that will help to build your own individual success.

That is positive growth!

| **Be a Visionary** |

How do you strategize and plan to do this? Being a visionary leader is really a couple of things. I have already talked about how, if you are happy with what you are doing right now, and comfortable, you are not growing. The only way to truly grow is to stretch yourself—mentally, emotionally, and spiritually—into an area that you are not comfortable with. When you are uncomfortable, you actually get to the point where you are able to gain new skills, learn something new, or adapt and change to accommodate or understand a new growth. When you grow, that is when you start to put out stuff in a new way. Putting out something new means you are leaning into a new thought process.

Becoming a leader and a visionary means taking risks. Change is about risk. Nothing happens overnight. You may take a risk in something and it doesn't work. You have to learn that some of the people who have received the greatest success in life, have actually been the ones who have taken the biggest risks in life.

They have risked so many things so many times, until they received that success.

As you acquire more and more grounding in what you want to do, you learn to listen and hear more. Listen to what others have to say about your vision. It doesn't mean that you have to apply everything they suggest, but if you are truly listening, then there may be kernels of truth that you may be able to apply as you make changes or tweaks. Being flexible in your plan means you are constantly assessing and reassessing what is not working. Taking that feedback in a serious way will assist in your own growth.

As an entrepreneur, you may have people on your team that offer advice. Now, it may not be what you want to hear, but if you are able to add them to your team, and everyone aligns with the ultimate goal, then listening to what they have to say is important. You brought them on the team for their expertise. Be a listening leader, and create a team in which you have listening teammates. As a visionary leader, you need to take responsibility when things don't go right. Step up and be honest about what didn't go well and the areas that need to be assessed based on that analysis. Create an analysis that gives everyone in your team an opportunity to share their thoughts, allowing people to also take responsibility for something that didn't work. Every event, marketing opportunity, or interaction you have with a client, is important for you to look at. Taking responsibility is critical for visionary leaders.

As a visionary leader, when I am going out on stages at various events, or mentoring someone, I am constantly filling myself with knowledge. I learn and then teach it to others; thus, I increase my understanding. A leader, who has a deep understanding or in-depth knowledge of their business and how to run it, will be able to coach others in it. You can imagine if you have someone in the field of selling trophies, essentially a trophy shop.

They might not know who their competition is, what the industry standard is for the materials being used, or the vendors that are cost efficient. They lack the knowledge about their business, but if they advertise themselves as an industry leader, then their credibility and trust with their clientele will be negatively impacted.

Understanding where your credibility and trust is with your clients, starts with getting feedback and reviews. They also provide essential third-party credibility to what you are saying and doing. On your website, for example, you might add client testimonials.

I have spoken, over several chapters, about how important it is to cultivate relationships. As a leader, being standoffish, not knowing your clients, and not being hands-on with your team is not a very good way to lead. A true visionary leader is approachable, and someone who is seen as rolling up their sleeves to get down to the grassroots level and work with the team. They are not sitting in an office and handing out tasks. If you lead by example, your team will be able to believe in your vision itself, and fuel that desire to achieve it. You all have examples within your experiences of places you worked, where you weren't receiving that energy from your leader, your direct reporting supervisor, the head of the company, or your department manager. As a result, you didn't really believe in what you were doing.

If you have a position where your manager comes to you for things that you feel they should be doing but are taking credit for your efforts, then it is time for you to move on to another role. You are not being groomed to grow in that role you are in.

Take an assessment. Be open to taking on another role or pushing yourself to gain knowledge, and create those interpersonal relationships that will help you along the way.

Another aspect of being a visionary leader is testing whether your current course is the right way to go. This is such a crucial element.

So, it goes from looking inward to assess your own journey to a more corporate level, and applying it on a business module. You are testing whether the goals, the mission, and the vision that you are putting out there, is constantly in alignment with your actions and what you are actually doing.

Your action items need to reflect back into what your vision is. What is your corporate responsibility on a larger social level in terms of giving back to society? If you come into work every day, and your energy is low, then be assured that your team players' energy will also be low. Starting every conversation in an energetic way will set the tone for how that person starts their conversation with the next person they encounter.

Communication is such a key component of a visionary leader. If you are positive, courageous, and encouraging and confident in your interactions, then that energy is going to translate into a positive and energetic environment.

You can imagine that if you have a boss and environment that are energetic, then you have a positive mental attitude. Now you can harness that positive mental attitude and mindset to build an energetic environment around you.

When you are presented with a challenge, and you want to say no to it because you feel uncomfortable, say yes, and figure it out instead. That is always a place to grow from. You may not have a solution right away, but it is always better to take on something and come back with a list of what you were able to accomplish, than to not take on the challenge at all.

Find someone that you can add to your team, who will help mentor you to that goal of accomplishing what you took on. Why can you not achieve something? It might be difficult for a variety of reasons:

- You don't have the skills.
- You don't have the people on your team with the skills.

Being a leader, you are still going to take the risk of accepting that challenge and taking a step outside of your comfort zone. You are pushing yourself and your team to reach that goal. By stretching yourself further than you thought you were going to, you can achieve that. As part of my teaching, I constantly pushed my students. They were able to achieve a little higher than what they thought they would have been able to achieve, if I had not been there to push them.

Stretching to attain that higher goal is going to get you closer to achieving it than you thought initially possible. Doing that, as a leader in a business, is challenging. It takes knowledge of a number of things, including an understanding of personality traits and how far you can push your team. It means being able to communicate in an effective and growth-related manner to your team, building everyone up so they can believe in your vision, and knowing what the benefits are and the return on investment. These components all together form the reason why being visionary in your purpose means being visionary as a leader.

| Push Your Accountability |

Why is it important to create a culture of accountability and be responsible about this? As I have gone through many different career streams, I worked in several organizations where they hired the right person for a position, but then they undermined them by micromanaging them or spoon feeding them. They didn't allow those people to grow.

Then those individuals wondered why there was no creativity coming from that position, or why there was such a high turnover in that position. As an entrepreneur, business owner, or manager, bringing people onto your team involves hiring the right people, for the right roles, to grow your job or grow your vision, and then letting them loose to create and harness the power of their minds. They can then come back to you with that creativity.

Focus on starting your meeting by discussing the ultimate goal and what everyone's role is. Having clearly defined roles and responsibilities within your group creates an accountability for that person's role within the ultimate purpose of your dream.

All of that is possible by masterminds, which I define as your core team that is working toward your vision. This asset of accountability that is within the mastermind, creates a purposeful journey toward your goal. There are certain things that are very important to creating that accountability.

The first component is to be clear about what you want to achieve. Write down your expectations. Clear communication regarding what is expected to attain that goal helps to alleviate misunderstandings and miscommunications within your team.

The second component is to be specific, goal-oriented, and to keep it measurable. I spoke about this and being able to gauge the analytics to determine, once you have obtained your goal, whether it was successful or not. These measures generate accountability through metrics.

If you are stagnating as a company, then you need to look at the energy within your team, which could be holding you back from reaching a higher goal level. You also need to be constantly assessing your goals to see if they are relevant. It can be easy to become derailed.

For instance, when you schedule a meeting, set the time period, the agenda, and provide all the key components for review prior to the meeting itself. Provide key leaders or guest speakers with the components that they need, in advance, so that everyone can arrive prepared. Have accountability within the meeting itself by having someone take notes and create a list of actionable items. People can then leave the meeting knowing what was covered and what they have to do as a result.

Check in with team members throughout the week, or on a specific date, depending on the terms laid out during that meeting for your goal acquisition or what you were measuring. It is about gauging what is on the right track to meet the goal, and what stage the deliverables are at. As a leader, you would check in with the managers as part of making sure that everything is on track, and to assess how they are doing.

Is there something that you as a leader can do to help them attain that goal? It is not about being hard on them or critical of them; it is about offering your services.

If you don't push your team and yourself to attain their goals, then they will remain unattainable. Not having the drive, ambition, and ability to motivate the members of your team to reach for that goal through effort, will make it unattainable.

Often, as a visionary leader, what you see as attainable may be seen as unattainable by your team. It is vital, as that visionary leader, to create the energy to share your vision and excite them to be able to believe in that, which will help to drive performance.

Key Takeaways:
- Getting to know yourself and your dreams will drive your branding to fit your purpose.
- To be a leader and visionary, you must be open to taking risks.
- Push yourself and get comfortable with being uncomfortable, to fuel your growth and reach your goals.
- If you don't push yourself, then the unattainable will remain just that, unattainable.
- Build a culture of accountability to fuel the growth of individuals within your team, including yourself.

Coaching, mentoring, and guiding are all going to be very paramount. That will allow your team managers to approach you as the leader, and to feel comfortable about their successes and challenges. This allows them to receive mentorship, which will build a strong team that has accountability to themselves, to each other, and to the business or organization as a whole. With all this in mind, let's talk about how being a badass in your life starts with action, and spend a few minutes wrapping up the conversation with your defined action points.

| Notes |

♥ PRO TIP ♥

anniejkoshy.com

GET READY, GET STARTED, GO!

"I have a hawk's vision when it comes to building my own success and that of my brand.

What's my motto? Be focused!

It's YOUR time!"

ANNIE KOSHY - AUTHOR
HOW TO BE YOUR BADASS SELF
A Guide to Using Your Inner Energy for Brand Success

CHAPTER 10
EYES FORWARD, MIND FOCUSED, HEART READY

| **Chapter 10 -** Eyes Forward, Mind Focused, Heart Ready |

As I finish this book, spring is just around the corner. That season is full of growth and renewal, from the flowers all the way to the animals. When it comes to personal growth, there is also a sense of renewal and change that is critical to the process. Part of my journey to be my badass self, meant reaching out for opportunities, not knowing if I was going to be successful or fall on my face. I can honestly say that I wouldn't be where I am if I hadn't invested in myself and jumped into situations that made me uncomfortable. That meant taking classes, finding mentors, and opening my mind and heart to new experiences. I stretched as a person, and it turned into growth.

Four years ago, as I was stepping out on my own and starting this business, I didn't know what was possible, but I had a vision of what I wanted to create. My vision fueled me, kept me motivated, and even when I didn't reach my goals on the first try, I learned and stayed focused on what I wanted to create. Auditions were places where I truly felt myself stretching as a person and an artist. It was here that I took on characters and broke barriers about what it was possible for me to play.

Now, I want to encourage you to grow. Throughout these chapters, I have shown you the ways that I have found contributed to my growth. Let's start by asking the hard question: Are you investing in yourself and your brand?

| **Invest in Personal Growth** |

If you're not growing, you're dying. To grow as a person means to constantly feed your mind with new thoughts and connections. If you are comfortable in what you are doing, your life, your job, your relationships, then you're not growing but rather stagnating.

Fortunately, this can be changed if you take action to get uncomfortable, because that is when growth is possible. How do you make something grow? First, you plant the seed, then you nurture it, feed it, water it, and provide the sunlight necessary. When it comes to personal growth, the thought is the seed you plant.

The constant need or desire to understand yourself and what impacts how you think about things is essential to getting rid of those blockages.

I also surrounded myself with people who were already better than me at specific skills, or who had already obtained success on the path that I wanted to follow. Listening and learning from them, then absorbing that learning and putting it into action, was critical to my growth. In order to grow as a person, you need to be constantly feeding your mind with new thoughts and connections, then taking action to spark change.

If you are happy with where you are, personally and professionally, then you are not really growing. All of us need to constantly evolve. If you plateau, then you are not just stagnating; you are actually on the decline.

Let's use a relationship as an example. When you first start the relationship, you are working hard to attract the other person and keep the connection going. You are spending time calling, texting, and working to learn about that person and their interests. Over time, you find that you become closer and set aside more time for each other. The relationship progresses to commitment. That may be when the relationship starts to suffer and go downhill. The thought process is that we won, we got the catch, or we made it, so we stop working or putting in the effort to nurture that relationship and help it to continue to grow.

The start of anything, be it a new relationship, a new mindset, or a new business, involves putting in the effort and focus to nurture and help it grow. If you want to keep it growing and healthy, then continue to bring that same focus and effort that you brought in the beginning. Every day, bring that same thought process and focus that you did on the first day. That effort is even more critical after a relationship becomes a committed one, or a business begins to grow.

If you notice a comfortable mindset settling in, then the best way to change is to start investing back into yourself and your personal growth to harness the power within you. Here are a few ways to invest in yourself that can reap major benefits.

- **Grow Confidence –** One of the biggest fears that people have is to talk about themselves in front of others. The more you invest in your personal growth, the more confident you will become in sharing with others and speaking about your own abilities and strengths in an authentic way.

- **Gain Knowledge –** I have mentioned throughout this book the importance of constantly feeding your mind. I have an insatiable need to learn. There may be a project that I take on, and once I do, then I go out and learn what I need to finish that project. There are mastermind opportunities, hiring individuals with the knowledge I need, or having someone mentor me through the process. Investing in your personal growth will help you to gain the knowledge to grow your thoughts and abilities. It is an investment in your own identity and personal growth. Don't use your free time sitting on the couch, filling your mind with thoughtless social media scrolling, or constantly binging the latest television craze. Instead, view your free time as your "me" time. Use that as the time to grow. Then you will be constantly doing things that will create a more robust personality, and one that will become a magnet for people.

- **Gain Skills and Market Them –** As you gain knowledge, you gain skills that you can market. When I became a photographer many years ago, the quality of my work was simply not there. In fact, I laugh now when I look back at those images. I was using rudimentary skills to create posters and other things. I didn't have the skills or knowledge to create the professional and crisp images that I create today. How did I get to this point? I recognized what I was lacking, and then went about gaining the skills and experience I needed. I taught myself, using online materials and courses. There is so much to gain and hone in terms of your skills, so I wouldn't even say that I am done learning yet. Still, I am learning and honing the skills that I need, to do my work in a more efficient way. Whether it is building my website, or creating social media posts, fliers, and covers that are in alignment with my brand, I am cost-effectively creating what I want, to express my messaging. All the branding requirements I have now, I didn't know how to do in the past. Putting myself out there, and learning, gave me marketable skills, not only for myself but also for my clients. It was all an investment in my personal development. I stand apart from all of my competition because I am a powerhouse. No one can look at my breadth of knowledge and experience, and pinpoint any of my skills that are not transferable to multiple areas in the digital and media realms.

- **Network Proactively –** One of the factors in my own success is my ability to meet, connect, and build bridges between these connections. When I meet people, I am not looking at what I can gain from them. Rather, I am focused on building a community. When I do my work as a form of service to others, then I am not looking to gain from that person directly, but I am looking to gain from the universe through other interactions. This is the number one benefit that I have gained from serving others. I was ridiculed by those close to me, including family. They said I was being used for my services, but I never looked at it in that way. I never even felt that way, until they gave voice to it, as they were coming from a place of lack.

I started to believe what they said was true. However, as I started to gain more and more knowledge about myself, and surrounded myself with like-minded people, I realized that my acts of service had come back to reward me with blessings tenfold, even many years later. I am filled with gratitude for those people who encouraged me to grow this mindset. Networking is the number one way to make connections with people. Every time you step out the door, you have an opportunity to grow yourself, and to grow those around you. Your interactions have the opportunity to open the door, and give you something to build on the next time you meet. Working and growing those initial two-second interactions is going to be your path to success.

- **Take Action –** One thing is to dream and plant that seed. Investing in your personal growth is taking the action necessary to turn a dream into a reality, and to really nurture that seed you planted.

| Learn to Say "No" |

I have come across several situations where I needed to say "no." When people reach out to me because they are intrigued with something that I have done, they aren't always willing or ready to invest in me. While you might be able to give things away for free, you have to decide who you are going to serve and who you are going to build up, and how those gifts are going to be a benefit. Part of my decision making in this regard is what will help me to grow as a person. I am very focused on my major purposes in life, and if something is not growing my vision or what I want to do as a person, then I have learned to say no.

If it is something that is stressing you out, exhausting you in some way, or undermining your self-confidence, then learn to say no. You don't have to give a long-winded explanation regarding why you are saying no. There are responses that you can give, which allow you to say no and still remain respectful. Here are a few:

- I don't have time for that right now.
- It doesn't align with where I want my company to go.
- This is not working for me right now.
- This is not convenient for me right now.
- I am not available for this right now.
- I appreciate you reaching out to me, but I am not able to take this on.

You don't need to ask for permission to say no. We often say no and take on an apologetic tone and body language. However, that is not really necessary either. If you are not ready to say yes, but at the same time, you don't want to say no, asking for time to think can be a way to consider the request and options without feeling rushed.

When I was offered a prestigious position on a board of directors, my first response was to not say yes or no. I asked them to share the information with me and then allow me the time to review it and get back to them.

If you are doing a project, and they approach you for something outside of the scope of that original project, you may want to continue to build that bridge with that person, yet not be in a place where you can say yes and fulfill their request. You do not want to put them off by saying no. One of the ways to assist, without taking on the request, is to reach into your network and see if you can offer them a viable solution that doesn't involve you taking on the task.

In another instance, individuals may want to collaborate on a project, but that project is not in alignment with where you want to go. Offer to connect them with someone in your network who would align more effectively with that project. It allows you to say no without burning a bridge in the process.

As a parent or family member, it can be most challenging to say no to our relatives. Having the experience and self-control to say no, in a loving way, knowing it will benefit them in the long run, is an important skill. Personal boundaries with family are an important part of that process. I had one experience where a family member wanted to give me money; in exchange, they wanted access to my personal affairs and a say in the decision making within my own life. The choice was to either accept the financial assistance and the strings that came with it, or to simply say no.

Ultimately, my decision to walk away and say no was based upon self-preservation, the ability to remain autonomous and an individual, as well as to show that I had the confidence and ability to move on without feeling bullied or pressured.

You might have relationships where you are dealing with conflict, but you simply cannot walk away, like those with parents, children, or a spouse. What is this person's relationship to you? The answer to that question might impact how you choose to deal with the negative or energy draining aspects of the relationship.

If a person means a lot more to you, then you are going to be more inclined to hear what they have to say, and to listen to their perspective, even during an argument. Here is a simple exercise, called pillow talk, that you can use to examine your perspective and feelings regarding an argument. Each pillow has four corners. In the first corner, you have, "I'm right and you are wrong." The second corner is, "You are right and I'm wrong." The third corner is, "You are right and I am also right." In the fourth corner, it is, "You are wrong and I am also wrong."

If you take each argument and flip it through these corners of thinking, then you are going to be able to take a look at how you are feeling about a certain position or argument. It does not mean that you are going to find the answer or how you feel right away. However, you are going to start identifying the energy drainers—those individuals that make you feel small and insecure. They are the ones that make you doubt yourself, your sense of purpose, your values and beliefs. Essentially, they are making you doubt the fundamental building blocks of who you are. Even if the relationship is one where you care about the person, the dynamics might need to change significantly. That starts by being willing to say no and stick by it.

For me, it was about being true to myself and what was important to me. Those are some of the reasons that I feel it is important to be able to say no.

| Pride, Clan, or Tribe – Immerse in Them |

I am a Leo, and those qualities are predominant, including a sense of loyalty and connection. Whether you call it pride, clan, or tribe, it is so crucial to surround yourself with people who are resonating with your vibe or energy, your mindset, and are building you up and supporting your growth. I had so many energy vampires in my life. What is an energy vampire? These are people that you meet who initially appear wonderful and even likeminded. The more time you spend with them, however, you start to feel drained. They may be putting others down due to their own insecurities, their own lack, and their own unhappiness. They give off negative energy, and that negativity will permeate into your world. These people can show up as co-workers, family members, or even close friends.

To invest in yourself, you need to surround yourself with people that vibe with you in a way that is energizing. Simply put, those who vibe with you are nurturing and enriching. There are people who also provide information that empowers or motivates you.

They give you the support you need when you talk with them to clear your mind. There are different members of your clan that provide different things, all contributing and serving different purposes. Not all of them are going to have the same goals. You will have different people to go to for different needs, and people will approach you for the unique qualities that you offer. Think of the different people who can help you regroup. All of us have been derailed by our own lives at some point, leaving us feeling unempowered and not feeling our best. But if you have people in your tribe who are able to sense that and help you get through that moment, then you will feel more and more empowered. How will you know the difference between people who vibe with you and those that drain you?

Well, who are the people that you spend the most time with? They are the relationships that you will have to examine closely.

- Are they helping you grow or are they depressing you?
- When you are with them, do you feel happy and uplifted?
- Is there something about them that is drawing you down or is toxic?
- How do they impact you, thereby changing your energy for your next encounter with someone else entirely?

If you have a powerful and empowering conversation, it will impact your next conversation in a positive way. If you start the day with these types of experiences, and continue them throughout the day, then you are spreading empowerment, and others will start to vibe at that energy level. This is what I am talking about when I focus on harnessing your inner energy for your brand success. When you have a positive mental attitude, then you are going to be energizing those around you and be energized by them in return. It can be the energy drink that really sets your day on the right course, and it fuels you. Plus, when you are mentoring others, they have the ability to mentor you in return. Your tribe is really the cornerstone of your experiences, both as a teacher and a student, which can be an incredible source of power and energy.

| Moving Beyond Your Past |

One of the biggest challenges for me as an individual was moving beyond my past. When you have a hurdle, burden, or past failure in your mind, it is important to move past that, but the process can take time. It is natural to initially feel frustrated, sad, remorseful, and discouraged after one of these experiences. One of the ways that you can get through all of that is to grieve.

Anytime you go through a change that is a loss, acknowledge what you lost, and grieve it. Perhaps a relationship or other experience didn't go the way that you planned, and there was a loss. Regardless of what it is, you have to grieve that ending and the loss associated with it. Once you grieve it, then you need to be able to forgive the people, the situation, and yourself. Your initial emotion may be anger at the situation or the people that caused it. Whether there was an intent to hurt or malign, if you hold onto that negativity, anger, and injustice, then you will be dragging yourself down.

Letting go is not easy, but it is so important.

By this point in the book, you have likely identified several things or blockades that are holding you back. Now you need to have an honest conversation with yourself about letting go of those things. It is okay to move beyond them and forgive. Doing so will keep them from negatively impacting your present. It is time to love yourself and forgive yourself, and then move on from that. Staying in that place will not allow you to grow your mindset or invest in yourself. If you can't grow your mindset or invest in yourself, then you will not be able to grow your brand or your business. Forgiveness is key to moving on.

Some people need to change their environment to let go. For instance, I had to put away certain pictures or reminders that referenced a negative place in my past. I grew up with a nickname that everyone knew me by, but one that I didn't like.

CHAPTER 10 | Eyes Forward, Mind Focused, Heart Ready

www.findyourselfseries.com

149

I finally understood why I didn't like it. That nickname was related to things that were holding me back, based on community and religious expectations of who I had to be. I realized that for me, that name was a trigger, taking me back to all the things that were weighing me down. I started telling people in my world, who continued to use this nickname, that I was no longer that person. Many didn't understand the change or need for change. But it was easy for me. The person who carried that nickname went away the minute a conscious change had taken place.

For me, I needed to create a ritual or a line that represented who I was, moving forward. I had to include that demarcation line in my interactions with people who knew the past me and who would also be part of my future. This is very helpful when dealing with people from your past, who will still be part of your future but are also associated with negative situations and emotions from your past. Essentially, you need to be able to clear the air to move forward from where you are right now.

| Be in Tune With Your Spiritual Being |

I have always been a very spiritual person. As part of my childhood, I grew up in an orthodox Christian family. It was something that I was surrounded with. When we are born into a family that has been steeped in religious tradition and ways of doing things, then that impacts us and how we view our community. There are also certain traditions and expectations that come from being raised in a specific community or region. However, that being said, just because you were born into a religion does not make you that religion. Being born into a family that follows specific rituals or norms does not mean that you are those norms. You have to practice something or have a great respect for a higher spiritual being or energy that is there. The actions have to come from you, regardless of what religious practice you choose to follow.

While this book is not meant to guide you down a specific religious path, I do acknowledge that there is a greater spiritual energy out there that can help to guide your life. In that sense, I am spiritual.

To me, my spirituality comes from my need to grow people through my acts of service, and is not really about going to a building, where I would sit and chant or say things according to a routine or ritual. My interactions on a daily basis with everyone around me is how I nurture and grow my spirituality. This is very important for each of you to understand. To grow your mind, you need to infuse your mind with thoughts that build the connection with your inner, spiritual voice. That connection with the universe or spirit will come when you are quiet in the mind. Mindfulness has to come when you allow yourself to meditate every single day, using this time to reflect and listen to the thoughts inside of you.

It is so important to have this meditation, to observe what is clamoring in your thoughts, what is holding you back, and what the messaging is that is coming through as you connect with that higher power. When you are taking the time for meditation in order to have a healthy mind, you need to have a healthy body as well. That means going to bed on time, fueling your body with healthy food, and stretching, taking a walk, and getting fresh air. It is about fueling your body, as well as your mind. There is an energy that comes about when you are balanced mentally, physically, and spiritually. If you are able to do this aspect of it, then the growth you will have on a spiritual level will be amazing, giving you the energy to grow yourself and the people around you, while in turn growing your brand and the business.

We all have the ability to be intuitive, but for many of us, we don't realize that those messages we receive are actually coming from our own inner selves. We are consciously receiving messages from our higher source, telling us, guiding us, and encouraging us to go down a certain path. That inner voice or gut feeling, those are messages for you, and it is important to pay attention to that. By staying open to them, you allow them to guide you toward what you need to do.

You can't do this on your own, so it is important to rely on your tribe, where you are feeding from and feeding into the energy created. It is such a powerful place to be when you are surrounded by like-minded individuals.

| Make Your Niche |

If you decide to copy others, then you will spend your professional life as a copycat. Whatever you do, make it unique to you. Whatever you do well, make it a marketable product. Find a lack or a need, and then work to fill it. Be specific about who you are going to market to before you start doing something that has been done over and over again. Find out about an area in your industry where services are not strong, and then offer the products or services to address that weakness. Then you can go to the business that may have been your competition, and offer them services and products to make their business better. That collaboration could lead to a partnership or other professional growth opportunities for your brand.

Most importantly, constantly market yourself—every minute, every day, and at every opportunity. Find ways to put yourself out there; educate potential clients to talk about what it is you are offering, and build relationships that are personable and that give you the opportunity to grow your worth and your business, with a competitive, powerful advantage over others.

Key Takeaways:
- Invest in yourself to build confidence and skills, and network.
- Move beyond your past to attain your badass future!
- Your niche needs to be unique, not a copycat of others.
- Allow your personal growth to include connection with your spiritual being.

Once you deliver products and services that cater to your clients and the customer service that sets you apart from your competition, and you are able to market that, then you have a win-win situation. You are now harnessing your inner energy to your advantage, and that is how you grow to be a badass person. May you continue to nurture and grow, to be the amazing badass person you are!

"Giving voice to the voiceless through thought leadership, photography, media and the arts."

Award-winning media professional, **Annie Koshy,** is a recognized multi-talented media and events personality, trained elite speaker, author, and emcee. Her work is highly applauded, as she has made a lasting impression within the arts, media, and events arena. Annie has gained a reputation for bridging opportunities for those in a variety of industries. Through her disciplined work ethic, aptitude for branding, and skill in business networking, Annie is a role model to many within the community. She holds senior management roles in several organizations in the capacity of Brand and Marketing Development.

As a published model with one of the city's premier modelling agencies, Annie has garnered mainstream attention through her commercial work. Most recently, she was featured in a lead role in a short film. A documentary on her life is in the post-production stages. Annie is the author of the book, How to Be Your Badass Self – A Guide to Using Your Inner Energy for Brand Success, slated to be launched May 2020. Annie is also a host with the mainstream radio station, Sauga 960AM, as part of their weekend fixture, The Source, where she engages in lighthearted banter and conversation. She is the Brand and Marketing Director for several million-dollar companies, and is called upon for advice and coaching on multiple levels. Most recently, she has been appointed as the Chair of the Board of Directors for a local artist-run organization in the heart of Brampton, Ontario, called Beaux Arts.

The icing on the cake is that Annie, along with 125 others, was part of a Guinness World Records attempt that was successful. In addition, along with the others, she is officially published as a #1 Amazon bestseller book in five different categories.

As a fine example of a multi-disciplinary woman leader in the community, Annie's story is inspirational and unique to young entrepreneurs and women. Her kernels of truth, and words of wisdom, are steeped in experience and cultural diversity.

Websites:
https://anniejkoshy.com/ / https://findyourselfseries.com/

Instagram:
@gtasouthasianmedianetwork / @anniejkoshy

Email:
gtasamnevents@gmail.com

Twitter:
GTASAMN

YouTube:
Annie J Koshy – Media Consultant

LinkedIn:
Annie K

FB:
Annie J Koshy – Media Consultant | GTA South Asian Media Network